Freedom Through Forgiveness

by Boyd Hopkins

WORDWIND
PRESS

Freedom Through Forgiveness

Published in Canada by
WORDWIND PRESS INC.
Saskatoon, Saskatchewan
wordwindpress@gmail.com

Names and details, in the stories used, have been changed to protect the identities of those involved.

Library and Archives Canada Cataloguing in Publication
ISBN 978-0-9917023-5-0

Layout & Design by Fancy Developments
Back Cover Portrait by Stuart Kasdorf
Cover Design and Photo by Shaun Salen
Printed in Canada by Globe Printers, Saskatoon, Sk.

WORDWIND
PRESS

Table of Contents

Acknowledgements

I would like to thank all of those who contributed to Freedom Through Forgiveness, especially those who attended the forgiveness seminar from which this book developed. You asked the questions that guided me as I wrote and allowed your stories to be used. I thank my wife, Jacqueline, who supported me and told me I was called to write this book. To her, it was not a matter of if I could do it but that I was called to do it. Further, I would like to thank Ed Strauss, Alice Berggren and Alison Uitti for the many hours of editing and proofreading. I thank Alison Uitti for her support and encouragement as my publisher. Thanks to Taylor Pfeifer and Michael Payne for their layout and design work. Thanks to Stuart Kasdorf and Shaun Salen for the photography and cover design work. Thanks to my son, Jonas Hopkins. He is the one with his head in the dirt. Thanks to the team at Spoken Word Ministries Association for the prayer, encouragement and participation during this long journey. Thanks to Gloria Olson for her typing.

Thanks to God Almighty for the many amazing experiences he has led me into during the years this book was in process. We saw many lives changed. May there be many more to come. God be with you as you engage the journey contained in these pages.

Boyd

Forgiveness Defined

Forgiveness is the act of giving up your claim to exact payment for a wrong suffered. More concisely put, it means "renouncing payback." [1]

Unforgiveness is defined in precisely the opposite way. When we choose not to forgive, it means that we *are* demanding that someone pay for what happened to us.

Prologue

Freedom Through Forgiveness is a book about forgiveness.

When we forgive, we say "Yes" as an act of surrender to God's grace and strength.

"Yes, Lord. I can't do this on my own because my wounds and my anger are too great."

"Yes, Lord. I surrender to Your mercy."

"Yes, Lord. I invite You into the place of my betrayal."

"Yes, Lord. I am ready to release those who have hurt me to you."

Through our heartfelt surrender, God's mercy begins to touch our lives with the redemption that Jesus brings to those who allow Him access to their brokenness.

In that moment, freedom begins.

The "if onlys"

Sometimes the injustice we feel we have suffered is so great that it has left us indignant and bitter, struggling to cope with pain and loss. At such times, the notion of choosing to forgive those who have wounded us may seem neither possible nor reasonable. The bitterness we carry can drive us to exchange harmony for division in our communities, families, churches, businesses, and friendships. Fear of being betrayed again often keeps us from embracing the forgiveness that can bring back the freedom we have lost.

People living with unforgiveness often suffer the "if onlys." "If only this person hadn't done this", "If only I hadn't made this mistake", "If only she'd kept her mouth shut", "Life would've been so much better if only..."

By soaking in the regret of what could have been ours "if only," we lose the ability to enjoy family, friends, coworkers, careers, and the sense of belonging they once brought us. As we become increasingly self-centered, focused on getting what we want rather than on what's healthy for all involved, bitterness eats away at our relationship with God, even calling our own eternity into question (Matthew 6:14-15). However we measure it, choosing to hold onto offense is a costly decision, expensive in terms of the anger, isolation, and bitterness that strip away our ability to experience love and be at peace.

Living wounded

Being "stabbed in the back" is an expression sometimes used when a friend betrays a friend. Picture it if you can. A person who lives with unresolved betrayal could be compared to someone trying to live with a knife in the back. Though it could possibly be done from a medical perspective, it would cost a lot in terms of pain and lost freedom. Focused on protecting himself from anyone or anything that might jostle the knife jutting out from between his ribs, our victim might try to act as though he was fine, but the knife would show any such claim to be false.

How about pulling it out? He would not be able to do it on his own because the pain he would cause himself in the attempt would be too great. Nor could he ask just anyone for help because removing the knife would require skills and resources that only a competent surgeon and a well-equipped hospital could provide. Even then, the decision to go through surgery would have to be carefully weighed. He'd have to ask himself, "Do I risk putting myself in the hands of a surgeon who says he can help me or do I just keep on living the safe, survival type of lifestyle I have become used to?" The first option would be scary because it would require him to trust someone with his wound, but it would be the only option with any real hope for positive change. Though the second option might seem safer, it would prevent him from dealing with the source of the pain and getting any permanent relief from it.

Holding onto unforgiveness is like that. The pain, fear, and anger of our betrayal are the knife in the back that destroys our ability to be truly intimate, both with God and with others around us. The pain is our soul crying out that something is wrong and that we need help to heal. Just as our imaginary man could not pull out the knife by himself, none of us can heal ourselves of the damage that betrayal has done to us. We need outside help of the kind that only God can give.

Even when it is not "fair" and we cannot understand why it happened, Christ's call to forgive brings a message of hope and redemption into our pain. Misunderstandings, slights, offences, and abuses are all a part of the human experience, and will continue to be as long as we are in relationship with others. But for those who allow the grace of God to become bigger than the sin that has been done to them, there is freedom to be had. The call to forgive is the only way to deal with the cause of the pain and regain the peace and freedom we were designed to live in. Those who have suffered betrayal will, at some point, have to make a choice to forgive so that the healing can happen. The journey toward that healing is what this book is all about.

Chapter 1

Forgiving is an Act of Faith

We must forgive if we are to survive

Often we become ready to forgive only when the pain of carrying what has been done to us finally gets so intense that we can't stand it anymore. As the injustice we have suffered is eclipsed by our need to embrace the way to freedom, forgiveness is no longer just about righting a wrong. It becomes a matter of survival.

I was teaching on forgiveness to a group of Pastors in the Democratic Republic of the Congo. Each of the 200 or so pastors gathered for the seminar had lost family and friends to violence in the aftermath of the Rwandan genocide of 1994. All were struggling to help their people rebuild lives shattered by war, murder, and betrayal. "We have to have this teaching. It is what our people need." The pastor who voiced these words spoke out of firsthand experience of the horrors of armed conflict and ethnic cleansing.

As the pastors shared stories of the horrors that they and their people had suffered, a sense of helplessness came over me. I felt as though I had nothing to say to them. How could a man from a country where there was relative peace come and advise *them* on forgiveness? They had seen atrocities and lived through trauma that I could only begin to imagine. Many had seen family members put to death simply for belonging to the "wrong" tribe. I could not see how my puny experience qualified me to address their staggering need and I voiced my sense of inadequacy before the group as we gathered on the opening day of our time together. I said I did not know how I could help them forgive because I had not suffered in the way that they had suffered. The silence hung heavy in the room for several seconds before a pastor from a nearby rural area stood and addressed me on behalf of all present, "You bring us the Word of God. It is enough. We cannot survive unless we forgive. If we do not forgive, the pain we have experienced will kill us. We must forgive and trust God. Only then can we be healed."

I had not seen it that way before. Sometimes the sins committed against us are too great for us to cope with. They poison our lives and strip us of hope. If left undealt with, the pain they cause can literally kill us. The only way to live through it and to heal is to forgive. Unless we release those who have betrayed us to the hands of God through forgiveness, and allow the Holy Spirit to bring an end to the pain, we will never find the freedom we seek. Many times since that pastor spoke those words, I have seen people place their enemies into the hands of God through forgiveness as an act of faith. The freedom it brings is nothing short of a miracle. Forgiveness is God's way of restoring the freedom we have lost. Those of us who live with the trauma and aftermath of betrayal need to experience the power of God's forgiveness if we are ever going to be able to come out of the darkness and begin to live again.

The Bible describes how Jesus came to bring about the greatest miracle in all history. Though the journey that Jesus walked was filled with pain, struggle, and constant temptation to take the easy way out, He held to His purpose and kept His focus. He did what needed to be done in order to make forgiveness available to all humanity. By doing so, He changed the course of human history forever.

For those seeking resolution to the pain and anger of betrayal, the writer of the book of Hebrews encourages us to remember that Jesus knows firsthand how difficult it can be to forgive and how hard it can be to trust again. We are not alone, though it may sometimes feel like it.

"Therefore, since we have so great a cloud of witnesses surrounding us, let us also lay aside every encumbrance and the sin which so easily entangles us, and let us run with endurance the race that is set before us fixing our eyes on Jesus, the author and perfecter of faith, who for the joy set before Him endured the cross, despising the shame, and has sat down at the right hand of the throne of God. For consider Him who has endured such hostility by sinners against Himself, so that you will not grow weary and lose heart."

Hebrews 12:1-3

Though we may not know what to do, God does. When everything else fails us, faith, hope, and the love of God will remain (1 Corinthians 13:13).

A way through the pain

One way or another, betrayal has to be faced and dealt with. It cannot be ignored. Betrayal that has not been adequately dealt with generates emotional pain as our anger at the one who has hurt us takes over the focus of our living. Dodging the issue does not help and pretending that everything is okay will not work. The Apostle John says that as long as we continue to live with hatred toward someone – even if that person is ourselves – we will walk in darkness, blinded, and unable to find a way out of the pain.

"The one who says he is in the Light and yet hates his brother is in the darkness until now. The one who loves his brother abides in the Light and there is no cause for stumbling in him. But the one who hates his brother is in the darkness and walks in the darkness, and does not know where he is going because the darkness has blinded his eyes."

1 John 2:9-11

The only way to gain back our sight, along with our ability to move through the darkness that hatred brings, is to forgive and let go of our grudges. If we are willing to trust God by forgiving, He promises to lead us back into the light and to restore our joy. The story of Mary[2], a woman who survived the Rwandan genocide, demonstrated to me the power of God to do what He has promised.

Mary was a Hutu woman who had married a Tutsi man. They had lived near their Hutu relatives in relative peace prior to the genocide, but when the violence broke out, Mary had watched in wide-eyed horror as her Hutu relatives came raging onto their property, pushed their way into her house, and hacked her husband to death in front of her. When it was done, they left her and her grief-stricken, traumatized children to bury the gory remains of their husband and father.

Finally the horror of the genocide came to an end. There were too many people guilty of murder for the existing justice system to handle. Under the influence of the Truth and Reconciliation Commission, her relatives admitted their guilt before a panel of judges and asked for forgiveness from the community for their terrible crime. With that, they were released to go on with their lives.

But Mary could not go on. She continued to live in the same house and every day she saw those who had murdered her husband living as though such things were easily put behind them. The anger over what she had experienced ate away at her like a poison. It destroyed the relationships she had once had with her extended family and neighbors, making her a prisoner in her own home.

One day, in the midst of her struggle, she was taken by a friend to hear a visiting pastor who had come to her village to speak. At the meeting, Mary heard a message proclaiming that, for those who had experienced betrayal and the pain that goes with it, the only way to freedom was through forgiveness. The pastor taught a simple method on how to forgive based on Jesus' words in Matthew 18:21-35. He described how she must confront her perpetrators. She had to tell them how deeply she had been wounded by what they had done and then declare forgiveness to them. She must say that she had put them in the hands of God and that what was behind them was now in the past. Once she had done this, she must re-engage in relationships with them as much as it was possible for her to do.

As the man of God spoke, the anger and grief began to rise in Mary's throat until she could contain it no longer. Her despair and anger surged to the surface and her sobbing became wailing as she collapsed into the dirt of the compound where the meetings were being held. Mary's pain was all-consuming. It was no longer a matter of getting justice for herself, but one of survival. She knew she could not live this way any longer, so she made her choice. She would do what the pastor said. Praying for strength, she dressed in her best clothes and set out on the long walk to her relatives' home. Confronting them about what they had done, she declared to them that she could no longer carry her anger. It was time she placed them in the hands of God and forgave them. What was done was done and she would once again be their sister and cousin, niece, and aunt.

A miracle happened. As Mary made her way home, the all-consuming anger began to fall away from her. As the days went by, the memory of that night no longer ruled her thoughts and the bitterness that had tormented her days began to disappear. She had let go, trusting God by placing her brokenness in His hands. What she experienced was nothing short of miraculous and she found herself beginning to look to God with anticipation instead of questions and anger. With her faith restored, she found herself increasingly filled with a sense that the future was bright. God had not left her on her own to deal with her pain, but in His love for her had come to set her free. Regardless of what had happened, she knew her husband was in the hands of God and she would see him in heaven one day. Mary was once again able to allow herself to love and be loved.

Forgiving is an act of faith that makes a choice, like the choice Mary made, to deliberately trust God with what has been done to us. The Apostle John says that we who obey God's call to forgive will experience victory rather than remaining victims because our faith allows God to intervene and to strip our circumstances of the power to destroy us.

"For this is the love of God, that we keep His commandments; and His commandments are not burdensome. For whatever is born of God overcomes the world; and this is the victory that has overcome the world—our faith."

1 John 5:3-4

Hebrews 11 says that faith carries a strong expectancy that there has to be something good ahead. When we act on that expectancy it pleases God because it allows Him to become the answer to our need.

"Now faith is the assurance of things hoped for, the conviction of things not seen....And without faith it is impossible to please Him, for he who comes to God must believe that He is and that He is a rewarder of those who seek Him."

Hebrews 11:1, 6

God does not just command us to believe. He calls us into faith by showing us who He is and asking us to trust Him with the burden of our desperate situation (1 Peter 5:7). When we do so, we give Him joy because we allow Him to carry us through our situation and into the freedom we were created for (Galatians 5:1). This is what John means when he describes our faith as a victory over what the world can do to us. With each act of obedience, each act of forgiveness, each act of trust, the faith we thought we had lost comes back.

We become convinced that we have not been left alone to deal with the betrayals and failings of life by our own strength and, though we may not know exactly what the future holds, we know *who* holds our future.

All of this comes through the willingness to step out in faith and trust that God knows what He is doing when He asks us to risk forgiving those who have betrayed us. As we surrender to Him, He takes the situation on Himself and brings the peace that only He can bring. It is not a matter of whether or not He can do it. It is a matter of whether or not we are willing to forgive and allow Him to do what He wants to do. The Spirit of God works tirelessly to draw us to the place of willingness.

Mary's story describes a very real act of faith. She took the risk of trusting God with her situation. The choice to forgive cost her everything she was holding onto, including her thirst for justice and her demand for revenge, but in the moment of forgiving her old life ended and a new life began. Her miracle happened once she was finally able to let God be God in the place where betrayal and trauma ruled her life. Like Mary, when we finally come to the point of being willing to give up trying to resolve the pain on our own and make the choice to put everything into the hands of God, it can feel as though something is dying within us. We may wonder how God can do anything with what we have to give Him. We may fear that He can do nothing at all. Yet this kind of surrender is necessary if we are ever going to let God become the strength we so desperately need. To take the step of trusting God, as Mary did, we need some understanding of God's heart for us.

Questions:

- Do you have a relationship you are fearful of trusting God with? With whom? Describe the risk involved in forgiving.

- How does the story of Mary impact the way you view your situation?

- As you pray, what is God asking of you about trusting Him with this relationship?

Chapter 2

Understanding the Heart of God

Jesus taught His disciples that there was no limit as to how often forgiveness should be granted, either by our Heavenly Father *to* us, or *by* us to those around us.

Peter came and said to Him, "Lord, how often shall my brother sin against me and I forgive him? Up to seven times?" Jesus said to him, "I do not say to you, up to seven times, but up to seventy times seven."

Matthew 18:21-22

Taking necessary action

God's heart is to heal and restore those who are in need. Knowing something of God's heart for us can empower us to do what needs to be done as we make the choice to embrace the way of forgiveness. Much of what I have come to know about the heart of God for His children I learned as a parent standing beside a diaper changing table. Cleaning up messy children is a necessary part of family life and each time my wife and I added a child to our family, we knew that along with the new baby would come plenty of messy diapers. We just accepted it as a part of the whole package of having a new child and did what we had to do. Never once did we stand over the changing table and scream at our children that there was a limit on how many diapers they could use that day. Never once did we sentence them to lie in their mess until the next morning so that they could "learn not to do it." We loved them and when they needed changing we changed them. We did so as often as they needed it done. As I stood by the changing table, it struck me that, like any healthy parent, God well understood how adding to His family would bring many opportunities to involve Himself in cleaning up after us. Like a father who changes diapers as often as is necessary, I learned that God has no limit as to how often He will forgive and clean up after us. All we have to do is ask.

God understands us

Isaiah says that our lack of understanding of God often holds us back from receiving what He has to give us. Standing by the changing table, I learned that God not only forgives as often as necessary, but He also understands why we do what we do and compensates for our weaknesses.

" Do you not know? Have you not heard? The Lord is the everlasting God, the Creator of the ends of the earth. He will not grow tired or weary, and his understanding no one can fathom. He gives strength to the weary and increases the power of the weak. Even youths grow tired and weary, and young men stumble and fall; but those who hope in the Lord will renew their strength. They will soar on wings like eagles; they will run and not grow weary, they will walk and not be faint."

Isaiah 40:28-31 NIV

God, speaking through Isaiah, asks, "Do you not know? Have you not heard? I am the everlasting God. I never get tired of loving you and living with you and I will clean up after you as long as you need Me to" (my paraphrase). Like a parent who understands what a child brings to a family both in terms of joy as well as the potential to create a mess, God understands who we are, and why we do what we do, better than we understand ourselves. There will never come a day when God throws up His hands and says, "I have had enough!"

God has no unrealistic expectations of us. He knows we will mess up our lives on a regular basis. According to Isaiah, youths *will* stumble badly. Old people will, too, for that matter. Just like parents with a new baby, God knows that everyone will make serious mistakes. He knows that we will all struggle with foolishness and immaturity, that we will all stumble and fall repeatedly, and that He will often be called upon to clean up after us. Knowing that, all He asks of us is to wait on Him and let Him be the help that we need. God has no illusions about our inability to perform perfectly, nor does He demand that we do so.

God lays it all bare

Just as a baby needs help at changing time, so we need God's intervention whenever we make a mess of our lives. Standing beside the changing table, I learned that changing the baby requires exposing the contents of the diaper, something never pleasant but always necessary. No matter how you work it, cleansing is a dirty process and yet God never shies away from what we have done as He seeks to make forgiveness a reality for us. Paul speaks of it in Romans 5:20 when he says, "The law was brought in so that the trespass might increase. But where sin increased, grace increased all the more."

He meant that God lays our sin bare so that what is laid bare can be dealt with. Like any good parent, God knows that He will get His hands dirty in the process of bringing restoration to His children. When Jesus went to the cross to take our sin upon Himself, God got His hands dirty. He did so because it had to be done. I never saw a baby who was able to change his own diaper. In the same way, God knows that none of us can deal with our own sin, and He is not afraid of involving Himself in our daily stumblings. He loves us and comes to us where we are at. Isaiah promises that whenever we stumble, all we have to do is wait on God and we will get the help that we need.

It is God's heart to restore

Standing by the changing table, I learned that God's heart is, above all else, about the restoration of His children. He is sensitive toward their pain and responds to every cry for help. An important thing to know about diapers is that sometimes they can cause little bums to get chapped and sore. When that happens, the baby cries out. I became very adept at being able to tell when my little ones were hurting and reacted quickly whenever I heard their cry of pain. Dropping whatever I was doing at the moment, I would be off to the changing table. Swiftly and efficiently, I would have the diaper open and removed, the wipes used, diaper cream smeared, baby powder sprinkled, and a new diaper put on in place of the old one – all to bring the joy back. I was often well rewarded by a smiling little face looking up at me, trusting and unashamed. Jesus' own words proclaim that God's every action, in touching our lives, is geared toward saving us from what would destroy us, and He often spoke powerfully of God's drive to restore us from the messes we have made of this life.

"For God did not send his Son into the world to condemn the world, but to save the world through him."

John 3:17 NIV

God's purpose is to save rather than condemn. The more we come to believe Jesus' declaration of God's purpose in our lives, the more it will change the way we live. Understanding that God's desire is to restore us, and that He is not afraid to get His hands dirty doing so, gives us hope and the conviction that our failings are not the end of the story, but rather the beginning.

"God demonstrates His own love toward us, in that while we were yet sinners, Christ died for us."

Romans 5:8

Christ is much more than a cosmic behavior coach who demands our spiritual performance. He is the expression of God's love. Driven by His love, He came to rescue us from total destruction and an eternity apart from Himself. Could He condemn us? Absolutely He could, but Jesus was clear that condemnation was not His purpose (John 3:16-17; Luke 19:10). Just as my reward for changing diapers day after day was the smiles of my children, so God is filled with joy whenever He has the opportunity to bring restoration to someone He loves. Rather than screaming curses at us just because we do what all children do, He sees our need and has taken the initiative to cleanse us and to bring our joy back. Paul says it well in Galatians 5:1: "It was for freedom that Christ set us free..." God wants us free. Freedom is what we were made for. Freedom is what we lost when sin came into the world. Bringing back our lost freedom is what God is all about. When we live in freedom, we live in the state that we were created for. This brings fulfillment to the heart of God in the same way that a child living in freedom brings joy to the heart of a healthy parent. That said, many of us are unable to see God in the way that these passages of scripture describe Him.

Gaining a healthy image of God

We all get our image of God from somewhere and, at times, forgiving those who have given us the image of God that we currently carry is a crucial part of our journey into freedom. Knowing God's heart will protect us from gaining the kind of flawed view of God that prevents so many from receiving what He wants to give. That means, in order to receive what God wants to give, our image of Him may have to change. If we see Him as an angry, vengeful God, we will hold back from Him, but as we come to understand His compassion and love for us, we will find ourselves more able to receive from Him the mercy He desires to give. We will also find it easier to forgive those who have betrayed us.

Cheryl grew up in an abusive home. The family maintained a good public appearance, including Sunday church attendance, but behind closed doors at home things were not as they appeared on the surface. Her father was a violent alcoholic who ruled with threats, intimidation, and physical violence. Cheryl survived by becoming a peacemaker. She developed the ability to read her father and to recognize the signals that warned of a coming explosion. She compensated for him, knowing that her father could not be trusted to do it himself. She learned how to defuse situations by deflecting problems and manipulating her father's moods. Whenever she could not defuse a situation, she coped by shutting down emotionally and riding out the storm until it was over. Then she would pick up the pieces, pull a peaceful veneer on over her inner turmoil, and go back to pretending that all was well.

Cheryl spent her young life in survival mode. As soon as she was able, she moved out and got her own place, desperate to leave the dysfunction of her home and start a new life that would be different from the one she had grown up with. She did not realize that when she left her old life, she would take her childhood training with her.

Cheryl wanted what she felt many of her friends had – a safe family environment and a healthy lifestyle, but it was not as simple as that. Never having been able to trust her father, Cheryl now found herself unable to trust men in general. Wanting a husband and the intimacy that she felt should be a part of such a relationship, she dated and was married. As Cheryl and her new husband sought to make a home together, they experienced the kinds of growing pains that many couples experience in learning to live with each other. But something more was wrong.

At the first sign of conflict, Cheryl reverted to the training she had received as a child in her abusive family context by shutting down emotionally.

She was unable to bring herself to risk confronting the issues that arose between her and her husband, so by the time Cheryl attended a seminar on forgiveness, her marriage was falling apart due to unresolved conflict.

At the seminar, for the first time in her life, Cheryl heard about a Heavenly Father who loved her enough to do everything He could to save her. Sitting in rapt attention, she drank in the message she was hearing of the Father's heart for His lost children and the love that motivated Him in reaching out to a world struggling with brokenness. In contrast, the primary parent figure that had ruled Cheryl's reality was her abusive dad. Though she had been to Sunday School and Church as a little girl, Cheryl's relationship with God had never been an intimate one and she had *never* related to God as a Father. Whenever they prayed the Lord's Prayer in Sunday School, Cheryl stayed silent, unable to pray with the others in her class because her image of a father had been so conditioned by the abuse of her earthly father that she could not even address God that way. When she did pray, she used the generic term "God."

After the seminar was over, Cheryl realized that she could not pray to a father because every time she used the word "Father" something inside of her shut down. She said she was hungry for the kind of connection with God being described at the seminar but she could not see how it could ever happen for her. She wondered if God could change her so that she could finally have the Father figure in her life that she had always yearned for. She was asked if she would be willing to forgive her earthly father and simply give him into the hands of God. She responded with a hesitant "Yes," though she made it clear she did not know how to do that and asked for help in how to proceed.

As she prayed, memories of her childhood began to come to mind – memories of being left on her own to survive the ravings and threats of her earthly father. Led to put her earthly father into God's hands, she forgave him for the years of torment and invited Jesus into the memories she carried. At her invitation, He came, and the presence of God began stripping away the fear and loneliness she had lived with for so long. A sense of peace enveloped her as her memories and the old image of her abusive father began to lose their power to prevent intimacy with her Heavenly Father. It was the beginning of a journey into healing that would transform both her marriage and her walk with God.

Like Cheryl, each of us has an image of God that conditions how we approach our spiritual journey. Things have happened in each of our lives which influence the way we see God. We may have had parents who, in their own brokenness or selfishness, created a negative image that we now associate with God. We may have been raised with an image of an impersonal God who lives far away in heaven and so we cannot believe that He has any real interest in us. Or maybe we were taught that God is a permissive, laid-back sort of God who is fine with however we live as long as we do not hurt those around us too badly while we do it. With no meaningful input into our lives, we have come to see God as uncaring, distant, and irrelevant to our daily living.

Many of us who grew up in legalistic church contexts were taught that God is an angry, demanding God. We live in fear that He is waiting to pounce on our failures with punishment and demands that we somehow pay for our mistakes. Our fear drives us to hide from contact with Him as we try to cover up our failings while struggling to live with the conflicting demands of perfectionism and our inability to perform well enough. Regardless of how we have come to view God, our image of Him influences the way we relate to Him.

God's goal is mercy

Jesus presented an intensely personal God who knows our faults yet whose desire and heart is to grant us mercy anytime and anywhere.

"But go and learn what this means: I desire compassion, and not sacrifice. For I did not come to call the righteous, but sinners."

Matthew 9:13

The Apostle John says that God is not interested in punishing us and that if we expect His punishment we do not yet really understand the nature of the love He wants to give us.

"There is no fear in love; but perfect love casts out fear, because fear involves punishment, and the one who fears is not perfected in love."

1 John 4:18

This passage simply says that when we expect God to punish us, we do not really understand God's heart for us. If we believe that God's heart is to punish us or to make us pay for what we have done, the negative fear that we live in will hold us back from coming to receive from Him the forgiveness we need. It will also prevent us from experiencing the kind of love-based relationship with Him that Jesus calls us to.

Being "perfected in love" means that we have come to know that God will continue to love us regardless of what we have done. We have come to understand that God's desire is to save us rather than to condemn us. We have to come to believe that God wants to redeem us and restore us to the freedom that we were made for (John 3:17; Galatians 5:1; Matthew 22:37-40). We have gained a conviction that God is for us, not against us and that His love for us is greater than the situation we have gotten ourselves into.

Once we become convinced that it is safe to approach God with our failure, we learn to waste no time in bringing it to Him so that He can set us free (1 John 1:9).

As we forgive those who have conditioned our image of God through the way they have betrayed us, God is able to change our image of Him so that we can trust Him for who He really is rather than what our fractured image of Him might suggest. A biblical image of God opens the way for us to engage God's call to freedom. My image of God began to change as I came to understand the heart of God more deeply during a devotional time one morning when a certain passage stood out to me:

"For God was pleased to have all his fullness dwell in him, and through him to reconcile to himself all things, whether things on earth or things in heaven, by making peace through his blood, shed on the cross."

Colossians 1:19-20 NIV

As the Spirit of God drew my attention to the fact that Jesus had made *peace* between God and me through what He did on the cross, a strong, clear thought was impressed on my mind: "I am not mad at you." It was suddenly clear to me that God was not holding my failures against me or demanding that I do something to appease Him. In that moment, I gained a new perspective on what it meant to live by faith. I understood that it was okay to take the risks necessary for my personal growth, knowing that God was able to handle my failings and weakness and that He would forgive me and clean up after me when I stumbled. As my fear of making mistakes disappeared, I was able to accept His invitation to grow into the future that He was calling me to. This insight came at a time when I was living with an undercurrent of guilt and failure in my own life. Suddenly I saw it clearly. If I wanted to understand what God was like, all I had to do was look at Jesus. After all, according to Paul, all of God's *self* was poured into Jesus and He was for me rather than against me.

He is pleased with us

Having had my spiritual appetite whetted by this new understanding of the heart of God, I began to delve into my Bible in a more focused way as I sought to gain a deeper understanding of what God was really like. During my search, a part of the Christmas story spoke powerfully to me as I read of how the angels came to tell the shepherds of Christ's birth:

"Glory to God in the highest, and on earth, peace among men, with whom He is pleased."

Luke 2:14

I was struck by the manner in which the angels told the shepherds that God was pleased with them even before they did anything to impress Him. His focus was on who they were as His people and He acted toward them out of the love that He had for them regardless of their social status or what they had done. The image of Himself that God showed the shepherds was that of a parent who takes pleasure in us, less for what we have done and more for who we are. I was suddenly aware of the pleasure that it actually gives God to forgive us. Just as I experience pleasure and relief when I save my children from potential harm, it makes God joyful when He is able to save us. Just as a healthy mother loves the baby in her arms simply because that little one is her child, or as a healthy father loves his child well before the baby can do anything but lie there and coo at him, so God loves us for who we are rather than for how well we perform.

I began to realize more deeply that I could not hide anything from Him anyway. He saw me and everything that I did – the good, the bad, and the ugly. Hebrews 4:13 says that nothing in all creation is hidden from God's sight. No matter how we may try to hide it from ourselves, God sees who we are and knows what we have done. He understands us better than we understand ourselves. We may try to fool ourselves but we cannot fool God. Knowing what we bring to the relationship, He invites us to be real with Him because getting honest is the first step toward true freedom.

Getting real

Getting real simply means becoming honest with both God and ourselves about what we struggle with. It means that it is time to stop pretending. We all have flaws, what the Bible calls "sin." Simply put, sin can be understood as the attitudes and actions that harm our relationships. In 1 John 1:8-9, it says, "If we say that we have no sin, we are deceiving ourselves and the truth is not in us." John goes on to say that "if we confess our sins, He (God) is faithful and righteous to forgive us our sins and to cleanse us from all unrighteousness." God invites us to come, hiding nothing, and to give Him what we have even if what we have to give is only the mess we have made of our life and relationships. He is able to redeem anything and everything. Jesus did not come for those who had their lives all together but for those in the greatest need. He came seeking relationships with those who were broken (Matthew 9:13). For those living in expectation of God's punishment, Jesus brought a message of compassion and hope stemming from His desire that we simply receive His mercy and live in it.

Questions:

- How has your image of God held you back from trusting?

- In what way does the diaper analogy impact your understanding of being in relationship to God?

- Is there someone who has conditioned your image of God whom you need to forgive? Who is it and in what way did they twist your image of God?

- How willing are you to forgive those who have hurt you?

Chapter 3

Understanding How We Are Made

Gaining a healthy image of God goes along with healing the brokenness, anger and pain caused by betrayal. It also involves an understanding of how God has designed us.

An inside-out approach to freedom

Two differing worldviews can affect our ability to live in freedom, depending on which one we adopt. The Christ-centered worldview is an "inside-out" approach that focuses on healing the source of our pain through forgiveness. The world-centered worldview is an "outside-in" strategy aimed at dealing with our brokenness by managing symptoms. The first is a proactive approach while the second is purely reactive. God designed us with the inside-out approach in mind. Through forgiveness we resolve the issues that cause the stress and anxiety so common among those living with unforgiveness. Only then can our return to health begin. I saw this kind of inside-out healing happen first-hand in a young man we will call Virgil.

Virgil's story

Virgil's life was a story of betrayal, failure, and despair. Though he claimed to believe in God, he had been trained in an outside-in model of living that focused his efforts on trying to fix himself rather than turning to Christ for the strength He could bring. As a result, he spent his time and resources struggling to overcome his symptoms and manage his guilt, living with a sense of his "badness" and unable to deal with the core brokenness behind his emotional pain. His misplaced focus prevented him from finding the freedom he so desperately sought.

At the root of Virgil's struggle was the legalistic paradigm of religion he had been raised in. He had been taught a quasi-Christian religious model that focused on his failures, demanding that he fix them in order to honor the God he claimed to worship. Convinced that he had no right to approach God or ask for forgiveness for his many sins, he saw forgiveness as something he needed to earn and which he could never quite attain. As a result, Virgil lived in constant turmoil, unable to compensate for the sins he felt he had committed. Always the guilt remained. Hoping that he would someday go to heaven, Virgil lived a life of coping with his shame daily while waiting for death to release him into eternity.

To make matters worse, well-meaning friends told him that he just had to work harder at trusting God, but he could not seem to do it. He just did not have enough faith. Along with the shame of his failure to live up to his idea of what a good person should be like, the ongoing stress of his unresolved guilt ate away at him and he began to withdraw from life. It didn't take long until he was suffering alone. Finally, one day, unable to cope any longer, he went to his doctor and was referred to a psychiatrist who began to treat him for acute depression. Virgil's psychiatrist did not see religion as a viable source of strength and said, "Keep your god. It's a good placebo, but real help will come from me." The advice backfired. Instead of lifting his burden, the doctor's declaration actually made Virgil's depression worse by further convincing him that he was so messed up that even God couldn't help him. As his sense of isolation and despair increased, it became obvious that he was losing his battle with depression.

His psychiatrist attempted to help Virgil in various ways, including legal options, as he sought to help Virgil gain freedom from his torment. "We can sue some of the people that betrayed you." Other well-meaning people told Virgil that he was not a bad person, that he was a victim and that he should not be so hard on himself. All of the well-meaning advice, whether aimed at minimizing his past or offering the promise of justice, failed. As he continued his slide into ever-deepening depression, Virgil became dependent on increasingly powerful medications until finally his life was completely defined by them. Spending every available hour in drug-induced sleep, he awoke one day to find most of his friends gone while only a few family members still saw him outside of his work place.

One day, two of Virgil's few remaining friends invited him to a talk given by a local minister on the subject of forgiveness. Not wanting to go, but feeling too guilty to refuse, Virgil agreed to attend. While he sat in the talk, struggling with his despair and regretting that he had come, something the presenter said struck a chord with him. Heart pounding, Virgil knew he needed to seek help through prayer after the session finished. With the help of his friend Virgil told of his struggle and did not minimize what he had gone through or attempt to explain anything away. Without criticizing or condemning him for the various ways he had attempted to deal with his dilemma, he was presented with a Christ-centered worldview. Helping him to see that his struggles were first struggles of the heart and that his healing needed to begin there, he began to realize that he needed to simply grant forgiveness to those who had betrayed him and to receive forgiveness for his own failings.

That day was life changing for Virgil. While it was not a magic moment that fixed everything in his life, it was a breakthrough and the beginning of a journey which, over the next six months, would see Virgil set free from the overpowering sense of shame that was the source of his depression. As he began to get increasingly honest with himself and with God, he began to learn how to give his guilt and pain to Jesus. He moved away from the belief that he had to pay for his failings before he could be forgiven and began to simply accept God's mercy whenever he stumbled or felt the old sense of guilt coming back. As Virgil replaced his old punishment-based worldview with one based on forgiveness and daily acceptance of the mercy of God, he found his energy levels beginning to grow. The tendency to sleep his days away was being replaced by a new alertness and a desire for activity. Whenever memories of his old failings returned, he prayed a simple prayer: "Jesus, because I belong to

You, my guilt belongs to You, too. I accept Your forgiveness and refuse to live in condemnation" (Romans 8:1).

Over the months that followed, Virgil slowly came off his medications. There were challenges as his body and mind adapted, but, with unresolved guilt and anger no longer the driving forces in his life, the day came when depression no longer ruled him and he did not need the medications anymore. He was free to begin the process of re-engaging a life that he had lost well over a decade before.

Depression can be an unforgiveness issue

As Virgil's experience demonstrates, stress caused by unresolved betrayal and unforgiveness can be a major cause of physiological breakdown leading to physical depression. Strategies such as demanding justice often only make the problem worse by entrenching us more deeply in our pain and anger. For people living with guilt or anger-induced depression, forgiveness *must* be *the* central part of the solution. Though there is often a time and place for medication in the healing process, medication cannot do what forgiveness does because medication is focused on managing the symptoms. Forgiveness actually deals with the core issue that causes the stress in the first place. In order to get our health back, we may need to forgive or receive forgiveness – sometimes both. This may be the only way we will ever experience release from the grip of the despair that rules our days and torments our nights.

Virgil's story is an illustration of someone with unresolved relationship issues who exchanged a world-centered, symptom management, outside-in approach for a Christ-centered, forgiveness-based, inside-out approach. As Virgil came to understand how God had made him, he learned to let Christ be his foundation. He began to surrender to Him the places in his life where guilt and anger weighed him down. As he allowed God in, He healed him. As he learned to let God have his burdens, He poured freedom into him, stripping away the crippling power of his old sense of guilt, shame, and anger. Key to his transformation was his willingness to forgive and to receive forgiveness. As he embraced the way of Christ, he came to understand that forgiveness is not about getting payback or justice or even fair treatment. It is about learning to give and to receive mercy.

How we are made

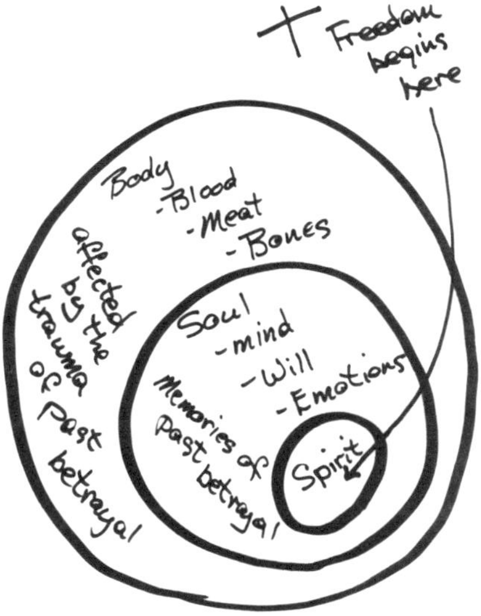

Making the shift from an outside-in symptom-management worldview to an inside-out forgiveness-based worldview requires some understanding of how we are made. Just as it is important for a mechanic to understand the workings of an internal combustion engine if he is to make effective repairs, or for a doctor to understand the workings of the human body in order to properly treat a cancerous tumor, knowing how we are made is important so that we can take decisive action to correct the brokenness in our lives. Paul gives us a concise picture of how we are made in 1 Thessalonians 5:

"Now may the God of peace Himself sanctify you entirely; and may your spirit and soul and body be preserved complete, without blame at the coming of our Lord Jesus Christ. Faithful is He who calls you, and He also will bring it to pass."

1 Thessalonians 5:23-24

We are three-part people. We are made up of spirit, soul, and body. Our soul is our mind, will, and emotions. Everyone has a mind, will, and emotions, and it is in this part of ourselves that we carry the memories and trauma of the bad things that have happened to us. (See the diagram.) Our body is our blood, our meat, and our bones – our biochemistry. Because of the huge influence that our hormones have on our emotional state, it is in the realm of the body that we medicate for things such as depression and the symptoms of other psychological disorders. Each part of us is interlaced with the others and so whatever impacts one part of who we are impacts all of who we are at every level of our being.

Comparing the outside-in and inside-out approaches to dealing with betrayal

The first facet of who we are is our spirit. The scriptures teach us that we are born spiritually dead because of sin, missing the relationship with God that we were created to live in. This lack of spiritual life hinders our growth and development until, at some point, we discover that no matter how hard we strive to do it, we do not have the strength to heal ourselves. We find ourselves in need of resources which only a relationship with God can give us (Romans 5:12).

The next facet of who we are is our soul - a part of us that is deeply affected by the state of our spirit. We were designed for a relationship with God that encompasses the mental and emotional identity of the soul. Without it we become turned in on ourselves, selfish in the way we relate to others and unable to engage in the kind of healthy relationships that we were created for (Romans 1:21; Galatians 5:16-21). When our spirit is filled with deadness, our soul reflects that into the way we live and interact with those around us. Conversely, if our spirit is filled with the life and love of God, it will reflect these virtues through the soul into our other relationships as well.

The third aspect of who we are is our physical body. Interconnected with our soul and spirit, our body remains distinct yet is deeply intertwined with the first two facets of who we are. Because of this interconnectedness, issues of the soul, such as unresolved guilt and anger, can affect our physiology, often manifesting as depression and other ailments. Just as lack of relationship with God affects our emotional and spiritual health, it also affects the degree of health that we enjoy physically.

The outside-in approach

An outside-in approach medicates the body, counsels the soul, and leaves us to pick our own spiritual power. With a focus on managing symptoms, it is by nature a reactionary approach which casts us back onto our own resources to overcome our problems. When it comes to treating issues caused by the stress related to unforgiveness, this approach cannot bring resolution because it does not address the core of the problem. At most, it can help us gain a limited, survival type of lifestyle. It cannot empower us to truly live.

The inside-out approach

The inside-out approach is very different in that it acknowledges the spiritual root at the core of our struggle, and begins there. Though there is room for medical treatment, including the use of medication, the foundation of this approach is dependence on God's strength instead of our own. Rather than trying to create our own spiritual power - a power that must be weaker than we ourselves are by the very fact that we created it - we are led to give Christ His place at the core of our being. In doing so, we begin to surrender to the power of the Holy Spirit as we learn to move ahead on the journey of giving our burdens to Christ.

As His forgiveness strips away our guilt and its associated stresses, the issues of our soul are resolved and the impact on our body observable. I have seen many who have lived in a state of survival return to health through this Christ-centered inside-out approach to dealing with unresolved woundedness.

This process of being healed from the inside-out is a process of being remade by God and begins by embracing the call to forgiveness. Saying "yes" to God's call begins a spiritual journey characterized by ever-deepening surrender to the Spirit of God. As God gains greater Lordship, He is able to give greater healing.

Exploring the process of surrender to Christ

Picture yourself as a piece of property and Jesus as the buyer who has just bought you.

"Do you not know that your bodies are temples of the Holy Spirit, who is in you, whom you have received from God? You are not your own; you were bought at a price. Therefore, honor God with your bodies."

1 Corinthians 6:19-20

Many may not be comfortable with the idea of being considered property but the image is a good one and it carries with it three key understandings. The first is that secondhand property invariably comes with garbage and repairs that need to be done. The second is that, when the new owner buys the property, he buys the garbage it comes with, as well. Thirdly, property does not clean itself up. The owner does that.

My wife and I experienced this firsthand some years ago when we bought property that the previous owner had allowed to become run down. The place was overgrown and had two sheds on the back end of the yard, both filled with broken lawn mowers, scraps from an old above-ground pool, old roofing tar, and other piles of junk. There was a lot of work to be done, more than I had anticipated. A little frustrated, the thought crossed my mind that the previous owner should come back and clean up some of the stuff he had left behind. Even as I thought about it, I knew it was futile. When I signed the purchase agreement, I had bought the junk along with the property. Suddenly I saw my relationship with God in a new light. I belong to Him. When He bought me, He bought my sin, too. Furthermore, I had been trying to clean myself up when what I really needed to do was just give Him what was now His and let Him do what owners do.

Giving Jesus access to the garbage

Let's expand the image a bit. Picture your "self" as a house with many rooms. You are an old house, an empty house, a house whose every room is filled with trash, mold, and rot. One room is filled with betrayal and another with the memories and trauma of abuse. There is a room with addiction, yet another filled with anger, and another packed full of bitterness. The commonality among the rooms is that they are all filled with the toxic after-effects of broken relationships. As the house is a picture of our whole life, so the rooms are a description of the places where we carry the guilt, anger, and shame generated by unresolved betrayal and failure.

As I processed this new understanding of myself as God's property, in my mind's eye I saw myself walking with Jesus through the hallways of my life. Suddenly He pointed at one of the bedroom doors. "I want to go in there." As He moved toward the door, I leapt in front of Him to bar the way, panic-stricken that He would see what I had hidden away. I implored Him, "Lord, just let me clean it up first." Jesus looked at me, His gaze piercing and filled with purpose, "You can't clean that up. All you can do is move the garbage around." What could I say? He was right. For all my efforts, I had never been able to clean myself up. Only

Jesus could do that and I knew I should trust Him to do it. Yet part of me was fearful of what He would think of me if he were to see me as I am. How could I open to Him the darkest and rawest parts of my life?

John's gospel speaks of Jesus as the light that overcomes the darkness and indicates that freedom happens for people who are willing to bring their darkness into His light (John 1:5; 3:18-20). I asked Him, "Lord, what do I do?" His response? "Go into the darkness and call out My name. I will come to you there." Rather than continuing the never-ending process of shoveling the garbage around while we try to cope with our brokenness, Christ wants us to give Him access to the place of our pollution. Though He *is* the Lord of Glory, the pure and spotless Lamb, He is also the Heavenly Junk Man (1 Peter 2:24). In order for Him to do what He came to do, we have to give Him access to the toxicity of the sin and betrayal that we so often struggle with alone.

Rather than leaving us to fix ourselves, Christ brings the power of His forgiveness into our darkness, cleansing and healing us from the inside-out. I cannot emphasize too strongly our need for Jesus to be given the access He asks for so that His Spirit can do His work of restoration. If left unresolved, the stresses we have hidden away will continue to spill over, polluting our lives and every relationship we enter. On the other hand, by yielding to Christ, we allow Him to bring His forgiveness to bear on the betrayal, trauma, and anger that have become the defining features of our lives. As the stress associated with such things is dealt with and swept away, the peace of God can take the place it once occupied.

An event and a process

The journey into freedom through forgiveness is just that – a journey. It is important to understand that a single experience of forgiveness is not all there is to gaining total freedom. Virgil's experience on the weekend (described early in this chapter) was only the beginning of his transformation. Though it was a major breakthrough that brought a significant amount of immediate relief, it was not a snap fix. Spiritual breakthroughs are similar to emotional breakthroughs in that time is needed to consolidate the gains made. During the prayer time, Virgil experienced a forgiveness *event*. He then went on to engage a forgiveness *process* that took him from that weekend into a day-by-day journey which continued over the next year. As he walked the journey out, Jesus healed him and set him free from his depression in stages. The more Virgil surrendered to Christ, the more he came to know the "God of peace" whom the Apostle Paul spoke of in Romans 15:33. He found that not only was God the source of the deep peace that he experienced during the weekend event but that, as he chose an active relationship with God, His peace both deepened and became a constant presence in his day-to-day living.

God deals with the whole person

Paul describes peace as a result, or by-product, of coming to live in the presence and power of the Spirit of Christ (Galatians 5:22). More than an event or a one-time thing, it is a lifestyle that will impact both our present and eternity. Paul's promise to the Thessalonian believers was that God would sanctify them entirely (1 Thessalonians 5:23). The word "sanctify" means "to set apart or to make holy." According to the Webster's Collegiate dictionary, the word "sanctify" means to "set free from sin" and "to purify", it carries with it a sense of housecleaning or life cleansing. It speaks of a journey that *both* begins *and* goes on as God brings His forgiveness to bear on our brokenness and makes a lifestyle of surrender to Him the defining reality of our lives.

The statement that God would sanctify us "entirely" echoes the understanding that God wants to impact every aspect of our lives. It flies in the face of the idea that forgiveness is something only for eternity. It makes the peace of Christ more than just a concept or a lack of struggle. As far as struggle goes, Jesus taught His followers that in this life we will have troubles (John 16:33). Yet, in the midst of the hard things that we face, there can be a kind of rest that is a by-product of being in the presence of God. We are not alone. God's strength can be our strength. God's presence can live in us where once there was only the pain and wreckage of failed relationships.

I grew up with the understanding that giving myself to Jesus had application only for the life beyond this one. I had compartmentalized God, believing He was only interested in the spiritual part of me. In my young mind, there was a room in my heart with a chair where Jesus came and took His place on the day that I said I accepted Him as my Savior. Once there, He just sat on the throne of my heart, doing little else as He waited for me to die. I am not sure that this was actually taught to me, but somehow I developed the idea that once I had said "yes" to Jesus, it was up to me to get through my life as best I could. At the time, that left me with about 75 years to kill as I waited to die so I could go to heaven. Convinced that God had no real interest in the details of my daily life, I had no idea how twisted my view of God and eternity really was.

We often fail to see God as interested in the whole person. Many of us view God as dealing only with our spiritual side while He leaves us to our own devices to deal with our physical, mental, and emotional needs. But it is not true. Contrary to my childish concept of God, Paul taught that God is *intensely* interested in who we are now, not just who we will be in eternity. He is fascinated with more than just our spiritual self. He wants to be involved in our mental, emotional and physical health as well.

Paul wanted us to understand that we serve a holistic God, a God who deals with the whole person rather than just parts of us. When God touches us in one area, His Spirit impacts our whole being in our ongoing journey into restoration. Beginning by calling us into a relationship with Himself, Christ restores us from the inside-out as, through forgiveness, He brings healing to every area of our lives. Our calling is simply to say "yes" to Him as His Spirit leads us on a journey of increasing surrender to His grace.

The potter and the clay

God knows what needs to be done in order to bring His restoration into our lives. The Apostle Paul calls us to ponder the image of a potter as we seek to understand how God works and how He can bring something good out of what we give Him to work with. The potter is an artist who works with clay. The clay is molded and worked by the initiative and creativity of the artist. The potter can even redeem a ruined piece of pottery by taking the damaged piece, throwing it again on the potter's wheel and collapsing the fragments into each other. He then remakes the whole into another usable piece. Nothing is lost.

The image of a potter and his clay is an illustration of how God, in His strength and wisdom, remolds the lives of those who surrender to His power (Romans 9:20-21). The heavenly potter re-crafts our lives in much the same way that an earthly potter takes flawed clay and reworks it until it is transformed into a vessel suited for his purpose. Like the potter, God is the artist who redeems and remakes broken human lives. In surrendering to Him the damaged and wasted parts of our lives, we give God the opportunity He seeks to heal and restore us from the inside-out. He gives us back relationships we thought were lost. He restores broken families. He gives a sense of self-worth where we had none. He will even restore mental and physical health as our unresolved stress is eliminated through the forgiveness He brings.

Though it might be hard for many of us to admit, this Christ-centered approach to living has often been lost in our world of today as formulaic religion so easily replaces relational faith. Increasingly large numbers of those who say they follow God find themselves living in spiritual survival mode, focused only on making it through this life so that they can go to heaven. Yet, only in returning to a Christ-centered way of living, and by engaging the journey of surrender, will we again find the freedom we have lost. In opening up the rooms of our soul and in giving Jesus what He finds there, our darkness is overcome by His light and forgiveness heals our brokenness. With Christ as the foundation of our freedom, life becomes an adventure rather than an existence. No longer tied to simply coping with our stresses, we can truly live!

Questions:

• Do you have an inside-out or an outside-in approach to life? Which method do you use?

• Think about the property analogy. What strikes you deeply in terms of the way in which you handle your relationships with God and with others?

• How does the idea of getting real with God and others make you feel?

Chapter 4

Restoring Priority Relationships

The GCPP

The GCPP stands for the "Great Commandment Priorities Progression" and illustrates the two kinds of priority relationships we were created for, with one flowing from the other. The first is the vertical relationship between God and us and the second is the horizontal relationship between ourselves and others. The second comes out of the first, and the first makes the second possible.

Forgiveness is about restoring the relationships we were made for. Priority relationships are our most important relationships and having them in order affects our ability to live at peace and relate in a healthy way to others around us. A baby's first relationship is with its mother. Without its mother close by, the baby's ability to live and grow is compromised. A husband's priority relationship is with his wife. Should his marriage fall apart due to neglect, the pain of his collapsing relationship will affect his ability to relate to his children, his extended family, his friends and co-workers, as well as his performance at work. Priority relationships are important because of the strength and life we get from them. When they become compromised or broken, they can only be restored through the giving and receiving of forgiveness.

Jesus' call to forgive one another is a call to love beyond the "give and take" kind of love that most of us are used to. He asks us to unconditionally love a God we cannot see as well as people we often do not know and many times do not even like. The Bible tells the story of a scribe who came to Jesus and asked, "Lord, what is the greatest and foremost command?" Jesus' reply revealed God's design for us by summing up the relationships we were made for in these words:

"'You shall love the Lord your God with all your heart, and with all your soul, and with all your mind.' This is the great and foremost commandment. The second is like it, 'You shall love your neighbor as yourself.'"

Matthew 22:37-39

Having our priority relationships in order empowers us to live in the way God intended us to. Also implied in Jesus' statement is the sense that when the relationship with our Creator breaks down, our relationships with each other are negatively affected as well. Many of us struggle to love others and, truth be told, we do not even love ourselves very well much of the time. The Bible teaches that our attitudes condition the way we relate to those around us (Matthew 15:18). If we cannot love ourselves, how can we love others? We cannot give to someone else what we have not experienced for ourselves.

Loving in the way Jesus calls us to in Matthew 22:37-39 can seem impossible and yet, over the years, I have been drawn to this passage time and again. It has helped me make sense of the seeming disconnect between the call to love and my own struggle with the brokenness and dysfunction that has so often affected my relationships with those around me. As I sought to understand how to love in a way that seemed to be beyond my ability, the Holy Spirit led me to another passage that gave me further insight into how we can live the impossible command to love God and neighbor as we love ourselves.

"We love because He first loved us."

1 John 4:19

We can only give what we have to give. In other words, we need to be loved before we can love. Loving in response to someone else's love became real to me the day that my wife first told me she loved me.

When Jacqueline and I began to spend time together, I had no pretensions to anything more than friendship, because I did not think she thought of me as being anything more than a friend. One evening as we stood on her front porch, the conversation was winding down and in a moment of silence she spoke, "I think I love you." With that one statement, she changed everything.

Taken by surprise, my response was not the smoothest and, not really knowing what to say, I mumbled something, hugged her and walked away.

As I processed her statement over the next few days, new emotions began to surface and I realized that her declaration had begun a change within me. I wanted to see her again. I found myself writing poetry, something I had never done before. I began buying flowers, jewelry, and planning evenings out. The guys I was sharing a house with at the time noticed the change in my behavior and commented on it. They said I "had it bad." I could not hide my feelings. I realized that I was in love with her, too and that my greatest need was to express it. That is what love does. It elicits a response.

Jesus' comment to the scribe who questioned Him reflected His understanding that the love we give comes out of the love we have received. It is during our time with God that His love pours into us and helps us to love beyond our normal ability to do so. As God shows us that His love for us is greater than our ability to fail Him, He helps us to see others in the same light. This experience of God's love makes true forgiveness possible, both the giving of it and the receiving of it.

Beware performance-based living – The danger of getting our priorities backwards

Having our Priority Relationships in order is especially important for those of us who struggle with performance issues. It keeps our relationships anchored in love rather than in trying to earn the favor of others. Performance-based personalities feel the need to earn everything they get. As a result, it is hard for them to either give or receive forgiveness because forgiveness is a form of mercy and cannot be earned, but only given. People who approach relationships on the basis of their need to perform believe that if they do enough, or present themselves in a way that people around them will appreciate, maybe they can be somebody. Driven by a low sense of self-worth, they think that the only way to gain the sense of value that they are lacking is by doing something, anything, in order to gain the approval of those around them. I call them "human doings" instead of "human beings."

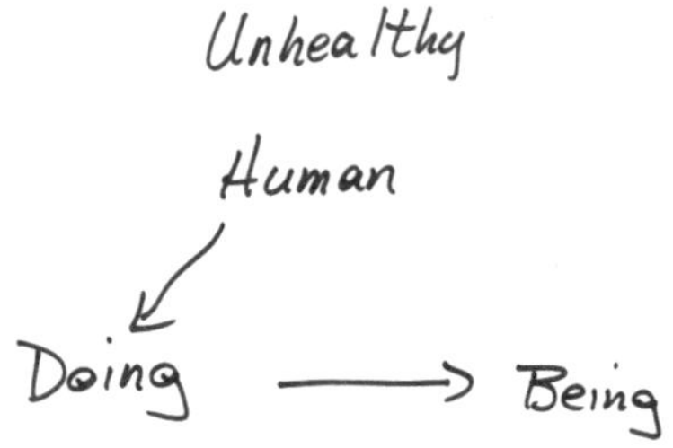

Because of his need to earn approval, a "human doing" lives with Jesus' two great commands inverted. He is constantly *doing* something to try to be somebody, striving to please God and others through his ability to perform. He hopes that he can gain a sense of fulfilment and identity based on his achievements. When a "human doing" cannot perform, or if he falls short of perfection in his performance (as he inevitably must), his sense of personal worth is degraded and he often struggles with anger generated by feelings of failure. Unable to gain the sense that he has God's approval, or the approval of anyone else, he struggles to feel loved because he feels he is not worth it. There is always a nagging sense of incompleteness and of having fallen short. As a result, people like this often develop a strong sense of self-hatred.

Performance-based living is selfish in its approach to relationships. When we build our relationships on our ability to perform, we essentially abandon dependence on God for dependence on "self" as we begin to make pleasing those around us our first priority. It may look good on the surface. I mean, after all, there are people all around us who are in need and we are called to help them. But the problem arises when we allow our time with God to be replaced by our selfish need to prove our worth. As our time with God dwindles, the strength we once drew from Him also dwindles. As we begin to neglect God, we set ourselves up for burnout and emotional exhaustion by increasingly spending our time and effort trying to compensate for our own weaknesses and the weaknesses of those around us. Increasingly, both our own need and the needs of those around us consume our strength and we begin to feel our emptiness grow. As this happens, we look around for other sources of strength and rest. Alcohol and other forms of distraction can begin to become a problem as we seek a quick fix for the stress we are now carrying. As we become increasingly self-focused in our striving to fill our emptiness, our love for others and for God becomes cold and empty. Often our spiritual emptiness brings with it a sense of loneliness and isolation that even surrounding ourselves with others cannot fully alleviate.

In contrast, a "human being" is a person who lives by faith. She is deliberate about keeping her priority relationships in the order they were designed for. She has found her "being" in her relationship with God and out of her "being" her "doing" comes. She lives with a sense of being loved regardless of her performance, and that love flavors how she reacts to those around her, whether she is at home, work, or church. She has found her identity in a relationship with God and she lives and functions out of that identity. Because her worth is based on who she is rather than on what she can do, she has the freedom to love herself and to be loved regardless of mistakes and failings. She knows that God's every touch on her life is meant to bring some kind of redemption. Instead of standing condemned, she is free to give God what she has and to take what He gives, including His forgiveness when she stumbles. This person lives with a degree of freedom that a "human doing" cannot understand because she knows her worth in the eyes of God and that sense of worth is the context out of which her daily living flows.

You may find yourself resonating with one of these two paradigms. Many of us who read this will remember a time when we felt free, but somewhere along the road of life, we slipped from a "being" identity back into a "doing" identity. We may wonder if it is possible to get back our lost freedom. The good news is that it is.

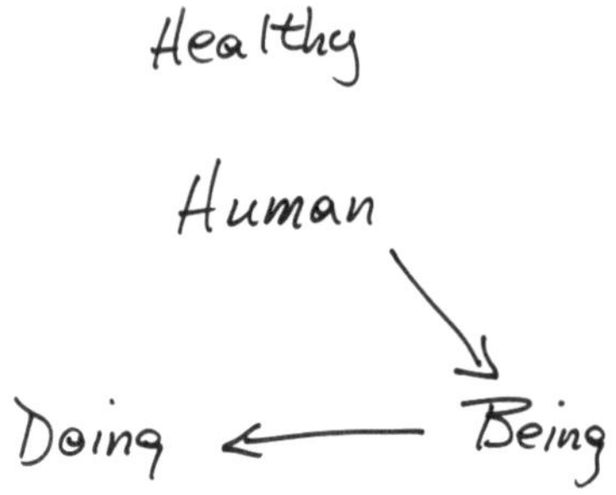

Go back!

The good news for those who identify as a "human doing," rather than a "human being," is that our orientation can be changed. We can gain, and regain, the freedom we were created for. The writer of the book of Revelation identifies the problem and points in the direction we must go:

"You have forsaken the love you had at first. Consider how far you have fallen! Repent and do the things you did at first."

Revelation 2:4-5 NIV

These words speak to those of us who have drifted from our priority relationships, whether with God, our spouse or other loved ones, telling us that we need to remember how we fell in love in the first place. Someone came along who was fascinating. They surprised us by loving us and their love changed us. We fell in love without even trying and, for a time, loving them back just seemed to come naturally. But, alas, the honeymoon wore off and we gradually fell back into old habit patterns as we got used to each other and began to take each other for granted. We began to neglect taking the necessary time to maintain and build the relationship and finally the day came when we realized that our affection for each other was gone. We had drifted away from our first love. It happens in human relationships and also happens in our relationship with God.

For those who have drifted away from God, Jesus calls us to remember what the relationship used to be like. He asks us to deliberately take time to think about how much we have lost and to go back to loving Him by nurturing the relationship like we used to. For some of us that might mean getting our devotional life back. For others it might mean re-engaging in a meaningful faith community. For many it might mean both. It can even mean temporarily setting aside "the ministry" to free up the time and energy needed to once again rest in God. Whatever it takes, do it! The book of James tells us that those who take action on what God's Word tells them to do are the ones who experience the blessing that God wants to bring into their lives (James 1:22-25).

Our priority relationships *can* be restored. We *can* experience God's love reinvigorating our love for Him and each other as it pours through us, empowering us to forgive. If we are willing to allow God's forgiveness to wipe away our wandering from Him, we can be healed of the selfishness that so often replaces lost zeal and love – a selfishness that often causes us to begin to see people as impositions rather than as opportunities to share what God has given us. We *need* our relationships put in order. As we make time to be loved by God, loving our neighbor will increasingly happen because His Spirit will give us both the opportunity and resources to do so. All of this calls us to some choices – ones that can be difficult because they require making real changes to the way we approach life. The good news is that even here God has not left us to do it on our own. He calls us to the necessary change. All we must do is respond favorably to His calling.

The Spirit-empowered choice

God is passionate about helping us to forgive and heal from the effects of betrayal. Driven by His passion to restore our freedom, God sets up encounters and calls us into places where we can engage the forgiveness that will set us free. God calls us. We can either say "yes" to this call on our lives, give Him what we have and engage the relationship with Him, or we can say "no" and continue to live in darkness. One way or the other, He calls us and a response is necessary.

Jesus spoke of our need for God's help in coming back to the relationships that we were created for.

"No one can come to Me unless the Father who sent Me draws him..."

John 6:44

He also spoke of our need to respond by receiving the relationships that God calls us into, including the relationship with Himself.

"But as many as received Him, to them He gave the right to become children of God, even to those who believe in His name."

John 1:12

A healthy relationship is a dynamic interaction. Someone reaches out, another responds, and a relationship is healed. Lives change.

We have to forgive in order to experience forgiveness

I have met many who struggle to say "yes" to the call of God. Often the blockage they struggle with is anchored in unforgiveness. Jesus bluntly taught His disciples that they could not experience forgiveness unless they forgave those who sinned against them.

"For if you forgive others for their transgressions, your heavenly Father will also forgive you. But if you do not forgive others, then your Father will not forgive your transgressions."

Matthew 6:14-15

"Pastor, that message hit me hard. You are saying I cannot be forgiven unless I forgive?" Albert planted himself in front of me and asked his question at the end of a Sunday morning presentation where I had been speaking. I responded, "Albert, Jesus said you cannot be forgiven unless you forgive. Do you think you can get into heaven without being forgiven?" Albert had not looked at it that way before and, as what was being asked sank in, he stared at me in silence. The muscles along the side of his jaw worked as he wrestled with his dilemma. At that moment, a younger man pushed into our space and Albert's attention was pulled away from me. The young man offered his hand to Albert and I stood back, watching these two men, struck by the similarities between them. One was a younger version of the other. Albert's eyes filled with tears as he took the proffered hand and was pulled into an embrace. His grudge had been against one of his own children. Healing happened that morning as Albert and his son, armed with a new perspective on forgiveness, heard the call of God, took action and forgave each other.

Jesus saw the need to forgive as so central that He built His teaching on prayer around it. In Matthew chapter 6, Jesus taught His disciples how deeply the Heavenly Father saw their needs, including their need to forgive those who had hurt them. He said that their prayers must come from the heart and warned them not to pray out of pride or for show. With these instructions in place, Jesus gave them a structure of prayer that we now call the Lord's Prayer.

"This, then, is how you should pray: 'Our Father in heaven, hallowed be your name, your kingdom come, your will be done, on earth as it is in heaven. Give us today our daily bread. And forgive us our debts, as we also have forgiven our debtors. And lead us not into temptation but deliver us from the evil one.' *For if you forgive other people when they sin against you, your heavenly Father will also forgive you. But if you do not forgive others their sins, your Father will not forgive your sins."*

Matthew 6:9-15 NIV

In the Lord's Prayer, Jesus called His followers to open in worship by praying, "Hallowed be your name." It was a call to let God become the central focus of whatever situation they might find themselves in, something especially important for those who have been betrayed and cannot seem to forgive and move on. By going on to pray, "your kingdom come," they were to acknowledge that their strength was not enough to fix their situations but were to call on God's kingdom and power to be the strength they needed.

Next Jesus called His disciples to pray, "Your will be done." Later Jesus brought out the full meaning of this prayer when He prayed in the Garden of Gethsemane, "Not my will, but yours be done" (Luke 22:42 NIV). We too have to renounce selfish agendas in order to allow God to be God in our situation. God may have allowed our situation to happen because He is working out a deeper purpose, or it could be that He is teaching us to trust Him as we let go of our demand to control how things work out. Regardless, we are called to leave the matter to Him by putting the one who has hurt us into His hands and simply committing to obey God's leading. Our willingness to let God do it His way allows Him to do what is best for us. He understands our situation more deeply than we ever will and He knows how to best resolve it. One way or the other, our willingness to let God do it His way allows Him to exert His strength on our behalf in times and places where our strength and resources fail us.

At the core of the Lord's Prayer, Jesus taught us to pray that God would forgive us our trespasses as we forgive those who have trespassed against us. Again, at the end of the prayer, He restated the importance of forgiveness by saying that unless we forgive those who hurt us we cannot ourselves experience the forgiveness we need. It is the only part of the prayer that Jesus restates. I have often heard people speak of how they pray and pray but just cannot seem to get peace, almost as if God is not hearing them. When you pray for a long time and get no discernable response it is easy to come to the conclusion that God does not care. Could it be that the problem is not God's hearing but that we are struggling with the blockage of our own unforgiveness?

That turned out to be the case for Albert. It was his unforgiveness that made him unable to be at peace. It kept him angry and cost him much in terms of the pain he carried over the lost relationship with his son, as well as lost time with his daughter-in-law and grandchildren. Albert was stuck and there seemed to be no way forward until the morning when he heard God's call and took action. In the moment that he forgave, the blockage was swept away and he got his children back, along with the joy and peace that had been gone for so long.

In Matthew 18:21-35, Jesus emphasized once again that forgiving others is non-negotiable if we expect to gain eternal life. Jesus was very bold in His teaching. He even went so far as to say that we can lose the forgiveness we have received if we refuse to forgive others. While I know this statement may challenge the theology of some, it is what the passage says. Regardless of how it meshes with our theology; if what Jesus says here is true, it carries a warning for those who have embraced His forgiveness selfishly and never carried through with granting to others what they have received from God.

Jesus tells the story of a man who was so deep in debt to his master that he could not pay it off. When the man begged for mercy, the master had compassion on him and forgave his debt. The man could not believe his luck! He was free! But instead of seeing the gift for what it was, an expression of compassion and love, he saw it as a way to further his own ends. Free of his huge debt burden, he could finally make some financial headway himself. So, rather than pass on the blessing he had received, he began to call in his own outstanding debts, refusing to show those who owed him money any of the compassion that his master had shown to him. He had not grasped what forgiveness was all about. When the master heard of how the man abused the gift he had been given, he was angered and reinstituted the old debt, casting the man into prison until he paid it off.

Using this story as a launching point, Jesus taught His disciples several key things about forgiveness. He taught that God is compassionate and takes joy in forgiving, valuing us above what we have done to get ourselves in trouble. He taught that forgiveness is to be received, not something to be used for our own benefit, but as something to be given away. He taught that when we truly receive God's forgiveness, we *will* take seriously our calling to forgive others from the heart. He warned against trying to masquerade before God, while trying to use what He gives for our own selfish purposes. He said that if we do that, God will reassign our old guilt and we will suffer the eternal consequences of it.

Many times I have spoken with people who experienced the initial joy of forgiveness, much like the man in the story, but then lost it again as they chose to continue living in the old selfish ways, refusing to grant to others what they had received with such joy. In the same way that forgiveness is not an option if we want to be free from the pain of betrayal, neither is it an option if we want to be a part of the family of God and see heaven one day. A person who refuses to give up his selfish grudges cannot bring his sin of hatred with him into heaven. He has to let go of it through forgiveness so that God can strip the sin from his life and save him. Forgiveness is a heart issue. It is a Holy Spirit-empowered choice and cannot be used for selfish purposes. It must be received in totality and given in totality. Regardless of how we feel, we must embrace the call to forgive because we cannot live in relationship with God, or each other, without it.

The great exchange

Jesus' warning that we have to forgive if we want to be forgiven seems to contradict the idea of the unconditional love of God. It is a question I have been faced with many times and those asking it make a good point. If God's grace is given unconditionally, why does Jesus say we cannot be forgiven unless we forgive?

As I prayed, asking God to make this clear, a picture flashed through my mind of me standing before God clutching a huge bag of trash in my arms, pleading for forgiveness yet unable to get relief. As I clutched the filthy, rotting mess closely to myself, I suddenly knew it for what it was. It was my offenses and my unforgiveness. Like rancid garbage will do when it is clutched so close for so long, it was making me sick. In that moment, the Spirit of God gave me a strong, clear thought, "Boyd, because your arms are full, you cannot receive what I want to give you. You have to be willing to let go of the garbage."

I had a choice to make. Would I let go of my grudges or would I hold onto what was making me ill? The moment I allowed my arms to go slack, the bag fell to the ground. With my arms now empty, I could finally receive the release that I was seeking. In the moment I became willing to exchange the bitterness of my grudge for the experience of His grace, He set me free. I learned that forgiveness means exchanging something old (our grudge) in order to receive something new (our freedom), just as Albert exchanged His grudge, along with the pride that had demanded he hang onto it, in order to receive his freedom and family back.

Forgiveness can cost a lot. Jesus gave up much when He forgave. Exchanging His place in heaven, He came to live on earth in order to save us (Philippians 2:5-8). On the cross, Jesus exchanged His innocence for our sin and guilt, taking on our torment so that we could receive His peace. Jesus exchanged His life for our spiritual death, and His willingness to make such an exchange made it possible for us to receive the freedom that forgiveness brings. We are called to this kind of exchange each time we are drawn to forgive, and the willingness to do so is the beginning of our freedom.

Questions:

• Are your priority relationships in order or are there specific relationships that need to be re-prioritized? Which ones?

• What changes might you need to make in your life to get your priority relationships in order?

• In what way does the "human doing" versus the "human being" analogy speak to your lifestyle and the way you handle your relationships?

Chapter 5

Breaking the Cycle of Unforgiveness

Someone once told me that the definition of insanity is doing the same thing over and over again while expecting different results. It is a good way to describe the way many of us handle ourselves when our relationships fail us. We often develop familiar and well-used methods of dealing with conflict or other relational problems, methods that become second nature to us. Through repetition, our ingrained responses to offense and betrayal become the cycle that we follow every time we experience a relationship failure.

When it comes to dealing with offense, we need to realize that doing the same old things repetitively will not bring about the change we are seeking. Unfulfilled expectations only create more anger and disillusionment within us. Like ruts in a muddy road, the more we use the ways we have become accustomed to, the deeper they become. Just as it takes work to free a bogged-down vehicle, it takes a deliberate choice and a significant amount of effort to break free from the relational ruts we have made for ourselves. Most of all, it requires a willingness to change the way we handle our relationships.

Jesus' call to forgive is a call to break out of our old, familiar, relational ruts by replacing our old cycles of behavior with new and healthier ways of dealing with offense and betrayal. What follows is a description of the "cycle of unforgiveness." It is intended to help us deal with betrayal and relationship failures by becoming aware of our patterns so we can make the changes necessary to gain our freedom.

Often when we are in a relationship and struggling with someone whom we feel has hurt us, the contributing factors to our situation can blend together into a mass of emotional confusion, making it hard to see a way through to a place of healing. It can be helpful to break the experience into a series of steps so that we can be intentional about examining the way we handle our challenges and become deliberate about implementing changes. To that end, I have put together the following models that I call the Cycle of Unforgiveness and the Way of Freedom.

The Cycle of Unforgiveness

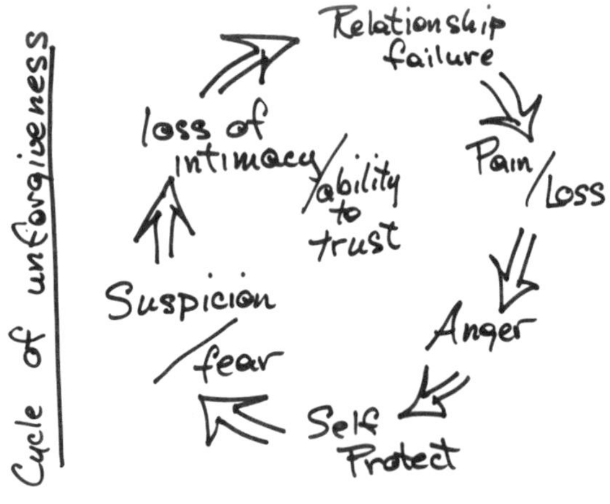

When we take offense

When we take offense against someone, we carry our offense until it is laid aside through forgiveness. Contrary to the old saying, time does not heal all wounds. Only forgiveness can bring true healing and, unless we deliberately choose to forgive, the person who has failed or betrayed us becomes the focus of our anger and triggers our cycle.

1. The first stage is the Relationship Failure stage. We experience a relationship breakdown when someone in an important relationship either openly betrays us or fails to meet our expectations of them.

2. The second stage is the Pain and Loss stage. The betrayal we have just

experienced takes something from us, such as the time we invested in the relationship or the trust we gave the other person. It could be that the hopes, ideals, and expectations that we had for our relationship, realistic or not, have been dashed. However it looks, we feel acutely the pain of the loss we have just experienced.

3. The third stage is the Anger stage. Unresolved pain and loss, if left long enough, become anger, and we may find ourselves asking the question, "Why did this happen to me?" Seeking revenge is often a temptation at this stage and we may become vindictive and punishing. In our attempts to pay back those who have caused us so much pain, we may use intimidation, threats, violence, avoidance, the silent treatment, or any number of other relational weapons as we express our anger. This can include using our anger as a "buffer zone" to keep distance between us and those who might hurt us again.

4. The fourth stage is the Self Protection stage. The old saying "Once burned, twice shy" applies here. Having been hurt and betrayed once, we are determined to protect ourselves from being hurt again. We begin to make negative choices, playing the "blame game" as we seek to justify what we are doing by blaming others, ourselves, and even God. As we allow ourselves to obsess over the hurt that has been done to us, we may develop our list of conditions that have to be met in order for the issue to be resolved. Should the other party get close to fulfilling our list of demands, we may find ourselves adding to our list in order to prevent us from having to actually forgive and re-engage the relationship. Just like we use anger as a buffer zone, we may also use our list of conditions to keep distance between us and those who might hurt us again. Accusation, self-justification, and the weapons from the anger stage are put to use as we seek to keep ourselves distant and safe from further pain.

5. The fifth stage is the Suspicion and Fear stage. Once we have been betrayed by someone we have trusted, the fear that it will happen again hinders our ability to re-engage new relationships. We become guarded,

distant, and suspicious of the motives of those we meet, and begin to lose our ability to open up as deeply or easily as we once did.

6. The sixth stage is the Loss of Intimacy stage. Conditioned by our past experiences, we begin to enter relationships expecting betrayal. On guard and suspicious of those we are trying to befriend, we have lost the ability to open up and take the risks that true intimacy requires, and so our ability to give and receive love dwindles. Our self-protective instinct makes us increasingly self-centered in the demands we place on those who would become friends. We feel alone, even when we are with those who are supposed to be close to us. The cycle continues to intensify as we move from relationship to relationship looking for a depth of love that we can no longer find because we have lost our ability to trust.

The cycle repeats

The more we use our accustomed approach to dealing with pain and betrayal, the more we become entrenched in it. During the course of our lives, along with new relationships come new failures and our tendency toward being creatures of habit will push us into repeating how we handled the last failure. As we experience the pain and loss again, the cycle repeats and the more it repeats, the more it *has* to repeat because it has become the only way that we have learned to handle those who fail our expectations of them. With repetition, things stack up. When we move to the next stage without gaining resolution for the stage we are in, we make things worse by piling unresolved anger on top of unresolved pain and loss. Imagine how an old car on a muddy road accumulates mud until its wheel wells are packed so tightly it finally grinds to a halt. In a similar way, stacking up undealt-with stages in the unforgiveness cycle will also finally bring our ability to live lives of fulfillment to an end.

The good news is that we can replace our old way with a new way. I call it the Way of Forgiveness.

The way of forgiveness

We can change the way we handle our relationships by proactively taking on a forgiveness-based lifestyle using Jesus' teaching on repentance and belief (more on repentance and belief in chapter 8 titled "The Surrender Process").

The Way of Forgiveness

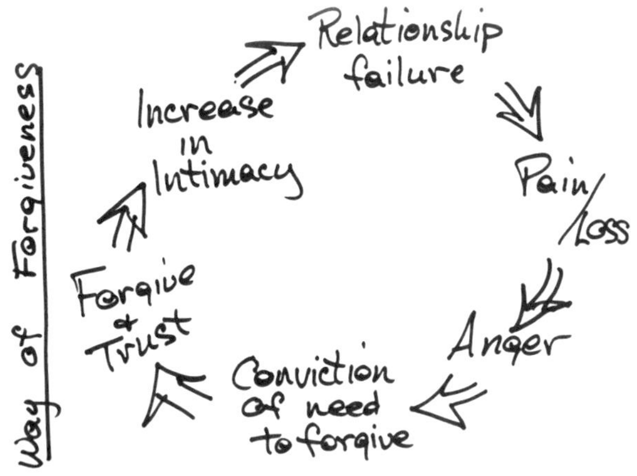

The Way of Forgiveness begins in much the same way as the Cycle of Unforgiveness.

1. The first stage is the Relationship Failure stage. Similar to the Cycle of Unforgiveness, here we experience a relationship breakdown when someone we care about either betrays us or fails to meet our expectations of them.

2. The second stage is the Pain and Loss stage. The betrayal we have just experienced takes something from us, such as the time we invested in the relationship or the trust we gave the other person. It could be that the hopes, ideals, and expectations we had for our relationship, realistic or not, have been dashed. However it looks, we feel acutely the pain of

the loss we have just experienced.

3. The third stage is the Anger stage. It is important to understand that anger is not wrong in itself and that it is the way we handle our anger that can become destructive. We can either let anger harden our heart as we make the choice to punish and self-protect, or we can allow it to motivate us to take corrective action, leading to a change in the way we handle ourselves.

4. Stage four is the Conviction stage. As we are tempted to let our anger drive us into the self-protection stage that we have become accustomed to, the Holy Spirit convicts us of our need to turn from the old way and to trust Him for a new way. (Mark 1:15). Our willingness to embrace what the Spirit calls us to is crucial if we are to gain freedom from our old cycle. Without that willingness, no change will happen and we will simply continue to pursue our old way of relating while we re-engage our old cycle. It is the willingness to embrace change, along with the calling of the Holy Spirit, which makes it possible to step out of our old cycle and into a new way of relating.

5. Stage five is the Forgive and Trust stage. Here we make a deliberate choice to step out of our old patterns rather than continuing on in the negative direction that we have become used to. We choose to make the selfless choice, rather than the selfish one, by taking responsibility for our actions and refusing to try to shift blame to those around us. In making the choice to take responsibility, we become proactive rather than just reacting to our emotions and situation like we normally would have done. In choosing to actively renounce the negative benefit we get from acting out our anger through punishing those who have hurt us, we also invite God into our pain as we choose to forgive. We release our conditions on those who have offended us, letting go of our demand to have things our way and putting the other person into God's hands by praying as Jesus taught us to pray, "Your will be done" (Matthew 6:10).

6. Stage six is the Increasing Intimacy stage. As we become healthier

in the way we handle our relationships, we gain a greater ability to be close to others and to enjoy intimacy. As our pain and anger lose the power to paralyze our growth, we become free to engage more deeply in our relationships. We become more aware of the damage that mistrust and cynicism can do to our ability to become intimate and we learn to distinguish between a selfish approach to relating with others as opposed to a self-giving approach. We become wiser and more realistic in terms of what we expect from people and, as a result, we are less easily disappointed when things do not work out the way we want them to. We become increasingly able to see people for who they are, rather than just what they can do for us. Bitterness and anger no longer control the way we enter relationships while we become more pleasant to be with and increasingly a blessing to others. Our practical everyday living becomes marked by freedom rather than constraint and bondage.

Repeating the way

Engaging the Way of Forgiveness will change the lives of those who choose to say "yes" to the Holy Spirit's leading. Deliberately making the choice to repeat the "Way" whenever necessary will prevent the crippling accumulation of anger and bitterness – things that would otherwise destroy our ability to be at peace, isolate us from each other, and bring on depression. Each time we say "yes" to the Holy Spirit's leading, His voice will become clearer to us and, as we consolidate those gains, we will begin to replace our old "normal" with a new normal, one that brings peace to our lives as our way of relating becomes increasingly healthy.

Questions:

- Do you recognize yourself on one of the cycles? __ Yes. __ No.

- Which one are you on? ______________________________.

- What stage are you at? ______________________________.

- Who are you on that cycle with? _____________________.

- What do you need to do to step off the old cycle? Are you willing to make the necessary change? __ Yes. __ No.

If "yes," freedom awaits. If not, you get to look forward to more of the same.

Chapter 6

Approaching Someone You Have an Issue With

Jesus gives us step-by-step guidelines on how to approach someone we are struggling with.

"If your brother sins, go and show him his fault in private; if he listens to you, you have won your brother. But if he does not listen to you, take one or two more with you, so that by the mouth of two or three witnesses every fact may be confirmed. If he refuses to listen to them, tell it to the Church; and if he refuses to listen even to the Church, let him be to you as a Gentile and a tax collector. Truly I say to you, whatever you bind on earth shall have been bound in heaven; and whatever you loose on earth shall have been loosed in heaven."

Matthew 18:15-18

The rainy season was finally over and the foliage was lush. Splashes of color stood out against a vibrant green backdrop interspersed with the bright red hue of the soil and the mud brick houses that made up most of the buildings around us. We were in central Africa, teaching a forgiveness seminar in a tribal conflict area. Looking around us, it was hard to believe that killing and violence were commonplace here in this natural paradise. In order to add a degree of safety to our gathering of community leaders, the local military commander had been invited to attend and had brought two truckloads of heavily armed soldiers to guard against the threat of violence from local militants.

As the teachings of Jesus on forgiveness unfolded, the commander sat fascinated, periodically scribbling notes in a small book. At the close of the event, it was customary for the senior dignitaries present to give the gathering a brief address. When the commander's turn came, he stood to his feet and addressed the gathering, saying that when first invited he had been skeptical of attending. He went on to say that he was glad he had come and that he had never heard teaching like this. Jesus' way of dealing with conflict, betrayal, and unforgiveness was so down to earth and practical that the commander declared it would help him in his very difficult job. He strongly encouraged the leaders present to take the teaching of Jesus into their villages and train their people in how to be agents of forgiveness in the communities of the area.

Jesus said to go to each other

According to Jesus, the first step in dealing with conflict and unforgiveness is to go directly to the person in private, just you and them.

Approaching a person one-on-one can feel risky, but it is the necessary first step for a couple of reasons. First, because it avoids the threat of public humiliation, it makes a positive response both easier and more likely. Secondly, it says to the other person that they are worth the effort you are investing in order to make things right between the two of you. The ideal outcome happens when the other person hears you, recognizes that you have a legitimate issue, and responds favorably. Jesus said, "If he listens to you, you have won your brother." Having heard you, he apologizes, forgives, or does both, and you get the relationship back. When this happens, it is important to re-engage the relationship rather than moving on. If the person does not respond positively, or if they refuse to see your point, go to step two.

Step two, according to Jesus, is to take a witness with you.

The witness is there to help communication happen openly and honestly, not to help you pressure the other party into admitting what they have done wrong. Knowing that emotions can distort the way we see things, the task of the witness is to listen to both of you and assist you in hearing each other clearly as you share your perspectives on the situation. If the meeting does not go well, the witness can also verify what was actually said between the two of you and be of help in preventing rumors and more confusion. If, at the end of this step, the person is still not willing to resolve the issue, go on to step three.

The third step is to take it to your Church (This step assumes that your antagonist is a member of the same Church. If not, take it to the leadership of whatever community that you *both* belong to).

We have to be careful about how we handle this step. Jesus was not talking about taking the whole congregation to the person's house to gang up on them, nor did he mean that we should draw public attention to the issue in the Church foyer. Taking it to the Church means that you get your Church leadership involved. The Pastor and Elders are responsible for the spiritual health of the Church family, just like parents are responsible to help their children work through their issues for the health of the family at home. They may confront immature behavior or voice their expectation that the people involved deal with the issue in a healthy way. One way or the other, the Elders bring to the situation a sense of community support and accountability as they help the struggling parties understand that the problem between them in some measure impacts more than just themselves (1 Corinthians 12:26).

What if, after all that, the other person still refuses to respond positively? Then the fourth step, Jesus says, is to treat them as we would an unbeliever. The question is, how do you treat an unbeliever?

Pondering this, it struck me that I needed to look at how Jesus treated unbelievers. As I re-read the stories of Jesus with this in mind, I was drawn to how He loved them. He was uncompromising on the truth and yet shared the gospel with them at every opportunity. He knew that if they were not willing to respond positively, He could not expect from them what they were not willing to give. With that perspective in mind, it became clear to me that He calls us to see those who are not yet ready to follow Him as He saw them, and to tailor our approach accordingly.

"Maturity" and unrealistic expectations

Treating someone as an "unbeliever" means taking into account the maturity of the person with whom you are struggling. Many seemingly unresolvable relationships have been the source of much anger and bitterness because of our expectation that the other person act with more maturity than they have. We cannot realistically expect from them what they either do not have, or are not willing to give.

Jeremy was Eric's assistant on a major community development project. As the job progressed, it became apparent that Jeremy avoided conflict and could not be counted on to communicate openly about the challenges his job brought him. Because his way of handling himself also affected the whole team, Eric spoke with Jeremy about the need for better communication, but saw no change. He took an intermediary to a second meeting with Jeremy and got nowhere. Finally, Eric brought the leadership team together in order to help the needed discussions happen. Nothing worked.

Driven by his fear of confronting conflict, Jeremy consistently made the choice to turtle up and do what felt best to him rather than what was good for the company. Finally, Eric's only option was to treat him like an unbeliever – that is, to not demand from him what he was not committed and mature enough to give. Rather than continue trying to force an unworkable situation, Eric was faced with the choice of removing Jeremy from his position, not because Jeremy was a bad

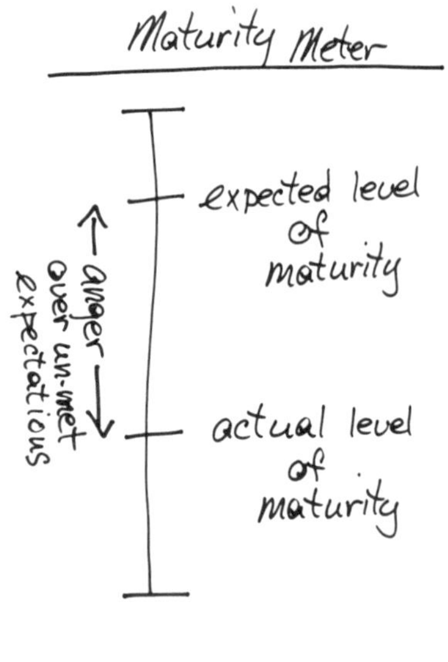

person, but because he did not have the maturity the position required. It was a difficult choice, but a necessary one, much like the one we may be called to make in situations where faced with step four of Jesus' process.

Though God stretches us because He wants us to grow, Christ never demanded maturity in His followers that they did not have. Going through the four-step process, as Jesus outlined it in Matthew 18, gives the person we are struggling with opportunity to demonstrate how mature they really are. It may also reveal that our expectations of them, due to their lack of maturity, are unrealistic. When we demand that those we struggle with be more mature than they actually are, it can set us up for disappointment and anger when they fail to meet our demands. By changing our expectations of them once it becomes clear that they will not respond in a healthy way, we can forgive them, put them in the hands of God and move forward.

Jesus' process for dealing with broken relationships involves a lot of time and effort. I have sometimes wondered why I have to put all that work into regaining a relationship that it would be so easy to let go of. Jesus' next words make His reasons clear.

"Again I say to you, that if two of you agree on earth about anything that they may ask, it shall be done for them by My Father who is in heaven. For where two or three have gathered together in My name, I am there in their midst."

Matthew 18:19-20

Simply put, Jesus taught that living in unity is the foundation of our strength as families *and* as communities. Though for various reasons we may have periods where we struggle with each other, Christ demonstrated as He went to the cross that any amount of effort is worth it if we can prevent our relationships from being permanently lost. Restoring lost unity is what forgiveness is all about and true spiritual power comes as we work together in unified relationships. When we restore a relationship, we strengthen our community. This is why the devil puts such priority and effort into destroying our unity. He knows that if he can turn us against one another, he can destroy our effectiveness and power as the family of God.

People who are always dropping old relationships and starting new ones never gain the depths of intimacy they are looking for. Communities that are always dividing and reforming become known for their instability. In the same way, churches and families that function in this way are unable to effectively proclaim the love of God because their divisiveness prevents them from becoming a safe place where people can heal and find a sense of belonging and growth.

In sharp contrast, when we learn to resolve issues and come back together, we both gain strength from each other and grow in maturity as we lay down our pride and give the Spirit of God opportunity to work through us. As we come back together after struggling with one another, we gain deeper intimacy with each other and with God. Giving and receiving forgiveness actually strengthens our ability to live in relationship as we learn to support each other rather than living at cross-purposes with one another. People like that get their prayers answered.

One-way or two-way forgiveness

It has to be said that our efforts at reconciliation will not always produce the desired effect and there are times when people will refuse to respond the way we want them to.

Charlotte's story

Charlotte came to my office seeking help for her marriage, "I've been asking my husband for forgiveness, but he won't give it. I don't know what to do.

Until he forgives me I'm stuck and can't keep growing in my walk with

God. How do I make him forgive me?"

Good question. The honest response is that we cannot force anyone to forgive if they do not want to. Neither can we force them to receive forgiveness. Even Jesus could not force people to receive forgiveness, though He freely offered it to them. By way of responding to Charlotte's question, I asked her to read the crucifixion account with me.

"When they came to the place called The Skull, there they crucified Him and the criminals, one on the right and the other on the left. But Jesus was saying, "Father, forgive them; for they do not know what they are doing." And they cast lots, dividing up His garments among themselves. And the people stood by, looking on. And even the rulers were sneering at Him, saying, "He saved others; let Him save Himself if this is the Christ of God, His Chosen One." The soldiers also mocked Him, coming up to Him, offering Him sour wine, and saying, "If You are the King of the Jews, save Yourself!"

Luke 23:33-37

Hanging on the cross, Jesus demonstrated that we can forgive and move forward regardless of how others respond. Two groups of people gathered to watch Jesus die. One group loved Him and grieved over Him while the other group was made up of the religious rulers and those who gambled over His clothes while mocking His gift of grace. He offered forgiveness freely to both groups. The former group received His gift of mercy, and eternity with it, even as the latter group refused what He gave. Regardless of how they responded to his offer, Jesus gave what He had to give and their response could not take away from His actions. As we shared this passage, it struck Charlotte that if Jesus Himself could not force people to respond the way He wanted them to, then maybe she was demanding too much of herself as well. Maybe, like Jesus, all she could do was make her offer and then continue to move forward with God herself, regardless of the response she got.

Charlotte prayed with me, forgiving her husband and accepting *from God* the forgiveness that she had previously looked to her spouse for. She placed her husband in God's hands and renounced her need to produce the desired result in him. As she finished praying and opened her eyes, I could see the peace that was now hers looking back at me. What better place for her husband to be than in the hands of God? Who better to deal with his stubbornness than God Himself? Charlotte was ready to move forward and she gained her freedom to do so with the realization that she could simply release her husband to God and let God deal with him.

Although it may be offered freely, forgiveness only benefits those who receive it. Jesus lamented over the unresponsiveness of the people of Israel: "Jerusalem, Jerusalem. How often I wanted to gather your children together, the way a hen gathers her chicks under her wings, and you were unwilling." (Matthew 23:37). Though He offered forgiveness to everyone, not everyone was willing to receive it. But He loved them and offered it anyway. We are called to do as Jesus did. Forgiveness has to be given and the other person's response must be left in the hands of God.

There are many reasons why people do not respond the way we want them to. For some, anger is their comfort zone. They may even like being angry. For others, holding onto an offense gives them a sense of control that they know they will lose if they choose to forgive. Some people simply want to punish and will not respond until they feel they have accomplished that. Whatever the reason, we need to learn how to move forward ourselves when someone does not respond well to our attempts to make things right. When we forgive as Jesus did, we do so primarily because it is an act of love and we need to understand that we are giving a gift to somebody who may or may not be ready to receive it. Regardless of their response we are called to give it anyway just as Jesus did and, if the person responds positively, we get the relationship back on a deeper level. If not, we do not.

Forgiveness does not mean forgetting

"How do I forgive when I cannot forget what was done to me?" Tommy's question came out of his personal struggle to move on from past offenses and he had taken to heart the old saying, "Forgive and forget." Having come to equate the two and because he could not forget, Tommy had come to believe that he could not forgive. He had not yet learned that in calling us to forgive, God has a deeper purpose than simply stripping us of our past memories. He wants to transform our past into a testimony that we can carry into our future. I shared Dale's story with Tommy.

Dale's story

Dale discovered that forgiving does not mean forgetting.

While in the process of coming out of an addiction to crack cocaine, Dale had been told by his addictions counselor to go to as many NA (Narcotics Anonymous) meetings as he could and to find a Church to attend as well. The idea was that he would stay so busy that it would help him keep from re-engaging his addiction. Dale chose our Church because it was close to his home and one of his friends had said that the pastor there was of the "down to earth" sort.

Dale called me up one day, asking if I would help him do his Step 5 in the 12-step NA program. I was unfamiliar with the program and asked him what Step 5 was. He told me that it was the part of his recovery from addiction and proceeded to read to me the purpose of step 5 from his 12-step manual: "We need to admit to God, to ourselves, and to another human being the exact nature of our wrongs"[3] Dale's intent was to simply confess to somebody all that he had done wrong and he was asking me to hear that confession. I told him I would be honored to and we set up a time to meet.

Dale arrived at my home carrying with him a stack of paper on which he had written everything he could remember about any time he had hurt somebody, betrayed someone's trust, or participated in destructive behavior. He sat in my living room and in a quiet voice read it to me page by page. What impacted me so strongly about Dale's confession was not just that it was raw, but how he did it. Without justifying anything he had done, he just laid it all on the table. When he finished, he set the last sheet down on the pile in front of him and there was a moment of silence as I tried to figure out what to say. Finally, I asked him how he wanted me to respond. He lifted his eyes to meet mine. "Whatever way you want to."

"Dale, I don't really know how to deal with what you just told me, but I know somebody who does. In order for me to talk about what you've shared with me, I need to talk about Jesus. Is that alright with you?" Dale looked back at me and replied, "I have a Higher Power." I realized by the way he spoke of his "higher power" that Dale's understanding of God was more conceptual than it was relational. "Dale, there's a power higher than your 'Higher Power'. His name is Jesus. Can I share with you about how He can help you?" Put that way, as far as Dale was concerned, anyone who could help was worth hearing about. His response was short: "Sure." Having received his permission, I shared with Dale a shortened version of the biblical story about Jesus being God's gift to people in need and how He came to seek out the lost and broken in order to restore them.

I spoke of Jesus' desire to bring forgiveness and healing into the places of greatest darkness in our lives. Going on to describe how Jesus paid with His own life for our guilt by dying on the cross and then demonstrating His victory over sin by rising from the dead, I shared Jesus' core desire: "Dale, Jesus calls us to experience the forgiveness and redemption that He made possible by entering a relationship with Him. Once we say 'yes' to that relationship, it allows Jesus access to our lives so that He can pour into us the strength that we need to live in freedom." When asked if he would like to begin that relationship, Dale's response was a simple "Yes," and we prayed together. It was evident by the time we finished our prayer that something miraculous had happened and I asked Dale what he was experiencing. "Peaceful, I feel like I'm lighter – like something heavy just lifted off me," was all he said. Looking into his eyes, I could see the work God had begun and that the light of Christ had penetrated Dale's darkness.

Once he had begun a relationship with Christ, the next stage of Dale's journey meant learning to give Jesus everything that he had to give – especially his failures. We spent the next hour in prayer giving Jesus all the things that he had confessed to me. At the end of our prayer time, I asked Dale how he felt. "I feel good," he responded. Dale had begun his journey into freedom by giving his brokenness to Jesus and accepting the gift of God's forgiveness. He experienced significant change as he learned how to give Jesus both his memories of those whom he had failed as well as his grudges against those who had betrayed him. As he implemented daily prayers aimed at offering Jesus his addictions and other sins, Dale began to experience the beginnings of a freedom that lasts to this day. He did not let his pride hold him back from what he needed to do. He just gave his sins to Jesus and allowed Jesus to strip away the guilt and set him free (1 John 1:9).

Several times over the next few months, as we spent time together, Dale commented, "You know what's so amazing? I don't live with the guilt anymore. I know what I did was evil, but the heaviness is gone." As I watched Dale come to grips with his new reality, I saw a man who had finally found peace. The guilt of his past, and the memories of what he had done, no longer ruled his thought life and dominated his days. Now when he spoke of his past, Dale spoke in light of how Jesus had set him free from it. Christ had redeemed everything, transforming the wounds that he had carried from a bondage into a testimony of God's grace and freedom. As with Dale, when we accept the forgiveness Christ offers, the burden of anger, guilt, and shame we once carried are replaced by God's grace. When forgiveness becomes real to us, we do not lose the memory, the memory loses us.

Tommy listened to Dale's story and came to understand that forgiving is not the same as forgetting. He was finally able to take the step forward, as Dale had done, and allow his past to be redeemed. He too had a testimony of God's grace to share.

Questions:

• Is there someone in your life that you are expecting too much of? In what way are they not living up to your expectations?

• Are your memories of what you have done a testimony or a source of guilt to you?

• How does the idea of inviting Jesus into the darkness make you feel? Why?

Chapter 7

Sin – the Great Divider

Understanding sin can help us understand why people do what they do to each other

Understanding sin is necessary if we are to understand what drives people to do the destructive things that they do to each other. Sometimes understanding what lies behind the actions of those who have hurt us can help us to forgive and find the freedom we seek.

Rory's story

Rory was struggling with the sin in his life and, although he did not call it by that name, his face mirrored the despair that he was feeling. As we sat together our coffee grew cold and forgotten while he named a litany of evil things he had done without sparing himself. "I am evil," he stated, tears running down his cheeks as he stared into my eyes, "I use people. I lie. I cheat. I steal. The woman I'm living with right now I only live with because of what I can get from her." He described habitual abuse and a lifestyle geared to his own survival as he looked at me out of tormented eyes that pleaded for relief from the suffering he was going through. One moment he wanted to know how he could get help and in the next declared that he was so evil he did not believe there was any help for him. His despair over the evil that had controlled his life, and destroyed his ability to have friends and family who loved him, was overwhelming.

As I listened, wondering how to respond to someone who was so blunt and honest in enumerating his sins and failures, it suddenly struck me. Rory was doing a confession. As he looked at me, his cheeks wet with tears, I found myself filled with a sense that God was calling this man.

Not knowing what else to say, I shared what I was sensing, "Rory, I think the reason you're experiencing this is because Jesus wants to forgive you. He's showing you what you need to give to Him."

I asked Rory if he knew Jesus. He said that he had heard of Him but it quickly became evident that he did not really know much more than Jesus' name, and that used mostly as a curse. With Rory's permission, I explained who Jesus was and how I believed the Spirit of Christ was calling out to him. I spoke of the love that drove Jesus in His purpose to save rather than to condemn and how all that was necessary was to be willing to let go of his old life and trust Jesus for the life He would give (John 3:16-17).

As he processed what I was sharing, Rory sat quietly. After several moments he spoke, "I was abused when I was young. I can't trust anyone. It's why I do what I do."

Lord, how do I respond? I prayed silently for wisdom. "Rory, are you ready to invite Jesus into the place where you were abused and where the evil lives?" Fear came into his eyes and he looked at me for a moment. "I don't think I can handle that," he spoke quietly, shrinking into his chair and slowly shaking his head.

I told him I was not going to try to push him into something he was not ready for. He sat for several moments in silence, with shoulders slumped and head bowed, tears dripping from his nose. Abruptly he looked up and made eye contact. "I think I'm ready," he whispered. I asked if I could help him pray and he said that would be good.

The scriptures teach that the darkness of sin cannot mix with the presence of Christ (John 1:4-5). Our prayer was simple: "Jesus, forgive me. Please forgive me. Please come into my darkness" (John 3:21). We prayed it several times and each time Rory got louder and more earnest as he leaned into the prayer, drawn deeper like someone finally getting the opportunity to drink the water he had been thirsting for. As we prayed together, inviting Jesus into Rory's darkness, we both felt the darkness break. It snapped like an over-strung wire. We both jumped and Rory let out an expletive. "What just happened?" he demanded. I responded that I thought he had just felt the touch of Jesus.

Rory began to giggle and then to laugh openly. Unable to stop himself because the relief he was experiencing was so great, he continued to laugh and chuckle for some time. When he was finally able to, we talked some more and I explained that this was what forgiveness was like and that nothing would ever be the same again should he choose to continue to follow Jesus. He had come broken and despairing over his sin. He left, giggling with relief, as the freedom that comes through forgiveness began to transform his life.

Rory had been abused and the abuse he had suffered had permanently damaged him. The sin done to him had conditioned him and made him into a user and an abuser himself. He had been so betrayed as a little boy that he had decided he could not trust anybody and made the choice to get what he wanted out of life whatever he had to do to get it. In his young mind, people were there to be used, just as he had been used. His life and actions over the years reflected the same kind of selfishness that his abusers had been driven by and, in the end, had left him filled with despair and self-loathing. But God had come looking for him and had begun to call him back.

As I watched the way God touched Rory's life that day, it was brought home to me how God values each of us for *who* we are rather than for *what* we do. In showing him his need for forgiveness, God saved Rory from himself and, in the midst of Rory's conviction that he was evil and unworthy, God gave him a sense of being deeply loved. There was nothing Rory did to earn the forgiveness that God gave him that day. He certainly did not receive what he deserved. He got what he was worth.

Only God can search a heart

Many of us, like Rory, do not know how to begin to deal with a lifetime of betrayal and sin but the Bible says that God knows us completely and can open our hearts so that the process of healing can begin.

"The heart is deceitful above all things and beyond cure. Who can understand it? I the Lord search the heart and examine the mind, to reward each person according to their conduct, according to what their deeds deserve."

Jeremiah 17:9-10 NIV

Someone once asked Jesus what kind of work they had to do to please God. Jesus responded that the work of God is to believe in the One whom He had sent (John 6:29). Faith in Christ allows God to bring His grace to bear in a life-changing way. Jeremiah spoke of how, as God lays bare what is in our hearts, God will go on to give us what our deeds deserve. Knowing that He would have to condemn us all for what we carry in our hearts, because of His love for us, God made forgiveness available to those who would receive it and washed our guilt away. When it comes to dealing with what we have done, our part is to invite God to search our hearts and then, in faith, give Him what He finds there. Rory's choice to trust Jesus with his sins and brokenness was the "deed" of faith that allowed God to reward him with the forgiveness that he so desperately needed (Jeremiah 17:10; John 6:29). As he responded to God's call to receive his forgiveness, Rory began a new life.

Worth everything yet worthy of nothing

The way God dealt with Rory illustrates the difference between "worthiness" and "worth." I first began to understand this important distinction during a conversation with my realtor. We had just moved to a new city, and my wife and I were out shopping for houses. We found ourselves looking at a particular house that had some damage and which

I thought was overpriced. Standing in the living room, I asked my realtor if he thought the house was worth what was being asked for it. His reply astounded me: "It's worth whatever anybody will pay for it." That statement left me staring at him with the strong impression that if I could wrap my head around what he had just said, it would change my life forever. And so it did.

Understanding the crucial distinction between worth and worthiness is important toward gaining freedom from our guilt. The cross of Christ is a two-sided reality. On one hand, knowing that we could never become worthy enough to earn back our lost innocence, Christ went to the cross and, in doing so, demonstrated our value to God (Romans 5:8). Like Rory, we might not be *worthy* since we have not done anything to earn God's approval, *but we are worth everything to God simply because of who we are.* According to the cross, we are worth what was paid for us– the life of Christ Himself. Rory's story proclaims that simple and life-changing reality. God forgives because He loves us, not because we have earned it. God pours out His mercy on us because of our worth rather than because of our worthiness.

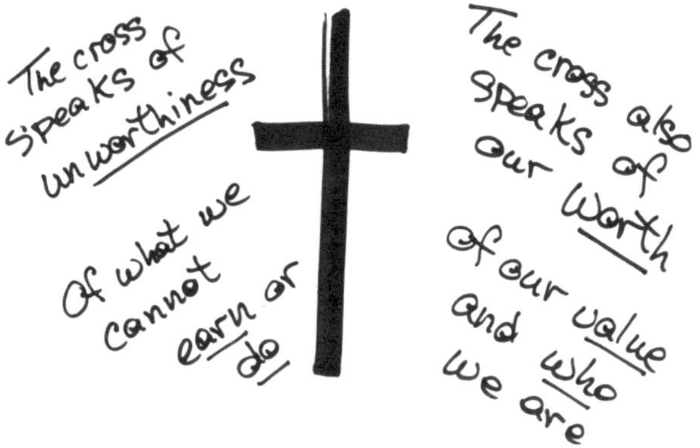

I have to emphasize it again: "worthiness" and "worth" are *not* the same. The former speaks of what we deserve while the latter speaks of our value to the God who made us. God loves us for *who* we are rather than for *what* we do. Our identity is not found in our failures and brokenness but in *who* we are as those loved by God. God never collapses *who* we are into *what* we do, nor does God *ever* equate us with the mess that we have made of our lives. Sin and sinners are *not* the same. According to the Bible, we all sin and yet we are all loved (Romans 3:23; John 3:16). The fact that we all carry some sort of guilt and failure does not diminish the love God has for any of us. God reaches through the sin to find a sinner in need of saving just as a parent reaches into a messy diaper to find a child in need of cleansing.

Performing for God cannot bring peace

Until we begin to understand our value to God, performing for Him can be a real temptation, driving us to try to mask our failures rather than take the risk of honestly showing God who we really are. We may feel that God deserves better and so we strive harder to be a good person who lives up to the standard we feel God has set for us. A performance-based relationship like this is both exhausting and hopeless, because there is always more we could have done or some area we have fallen short in, and so we end up living with peace as an unattainable goal rather than as our daily reality. I spent a lot of years trying to clean up my act but could never gain a sense of having succeeded. When I think about the impossibility of attaining perfection through performance, I am reminded of Joseph.

Joseph's story

Joseph was a bodybuilder and a top athlete. He had chiseled features and the most incredible physique of anyone I had ever met. One day he took me to the gym to work out and I was struck by the way Joseph interacted with the mirrored walls that allowed the athletes to view their progress. He could not seem to see his success. All he could see were his flaws. Standing before the mirrors and flexing, he pointed out areas he needed to work on, "Hmmm. Too thick here. Need to build up here. Gotta move this over here." Never satisfied with himself, his greatest frustration was that the mirrors showed him his inability to achieve the perfection that he sought. It reminded me of the Ten Commandments.

The Ten Commandments are like the mirrors at the gym. They make us aware of our failures and sins every time we come into contact with them. Because they show what a perfect life should look like, they highlight our imperfections whenever we compare our lives to what they demand (Romans 3:20).

The Commandments, otherwise referred to as "the law", are a powerful tool that can be used to serve different purposes. Both God and the devil use the Commandments for their own ends. The devil uses the law to condemn. He uses it to highlight our flaws by drawing attention to our failures and focusing us on our weaknesses. He wants to enhance our sense of unworthiness before God by increasing our sense of hopelessness over our inability to perform according to the demands of the law. His goal is to drive us into depression and to paralyze us with despair so that we will give up on attaining a relationship with God and lose any hope of freedom and worth.

In sharp contrast to the way the devil works, God uses the law redemptively. Rather than condemning us for our failures, He uses the commandments to show us our inability to live up to what the law requires. God knows that we can never find the peace we were made for by trying to follow the letter of the law. Rather than demanding our performance, He actually calls us to stop performing and, at the same time, He exposes our failures so that He can lift them off our lives through forgiveness. Romans 5:20-21 says, "The law came in so that the transgression would increase, but where sin increased, grace abounded all the more. So that, as sin reigned in death, even so grace would reign through righteousness to eternal life through Jesus Christ our Lord." Paul specifically states that it is in the place of greatest sin that the mercy of God is most powerfully experienced.

Knowing God's purpose in showing us our sin gives us the freedom to accept His forgiveness and stop striving for a perfection we can never reach. As much as God is not interested in our performance, He is totally enthralled by our surrender to His grace. It allows Him to do what He came to do by giving us what we need most desperately – His mercy. Jesus always went to places where sin and brokenness were the greatest. He went into lives that were filled with betrayal, bitterness, and despair. He always called sin for what it was, often quite bluntly, and yet people sensed His love for them, often responding by begging Him to show them what they must do. He always did and, in doing so, He showed them what living by His mercy could really mean for their lives.

Sin destroys relationships

When God created the first people, He intended humanity to live in innocence and freedom. Then sin entered the world and with sin came guilt. Because God had not meant for us to live in a sinful world, He did not build into us the ability to carry guilt. It is why we do not carry it well and defeating the power of guilt to condemn us is the reason Jesus had to come to do what He did on the cross.

There are two levels of relationship that sin destroys. (Matthew 22:37-40). The first is the relationship with God himself. The second is a result of the first – our ability to selflessly love one another.

The moment sin entered the human experience, it did what sin does by shattering every relationship that it touched. Guilt and shame became the driving motivators, changing the way Adam and Eve related to God and to each other. Rather than looking forward to time with their Creator, they now began to hide from the presence of God. When God sought them out and asked what they had done, Adam reacted defensively. He spoke out of his shame and pain as he tried to compensate for his newly-acquired sense of guilt that stemmed from his just-awakened self-centeredness. He began to blame others, much like an immature child caught doing something wrong blames those around him so he can dodge responsibility for his actions. Adam accused both God and his wife – God for creating the problem in the first place by giving him the woman, and his wife for handing him the forbidden fruit (Genesis 3:9-12). His newfound guilt wiped out his sense of freedom, brought division into his marriage, and set Adam against the God who loved him above all else.

Sin is an old word. Sin is a blunt word. Sin is what abusers do. Sin is what abuse victims suffer from. Sin happens when someone, out of selfishness, betrays a trust. Sin finds expression each time a child throws himself on the ground screaming that he wants his own way, or sulks in the corner because things did not go the way she wanted them to go. Sin manifests through things like a driver screaming curses at other drivers on the freeway, a friend attacking other friends in a drunken rage, character assassination through gossip, and a multitude of other selfish actions. Sin is what destroys relationships between us, each other, and God. God hates sin because of the division it causes between Him and those He loves. When we speak about sin, we speak of the damage that sin has done, something only forgiveness can address. Sin is like snake venom. It is relational poison.

Snake bitten

As a boy I enjoyed western novels. One of my favorite western writers often included life-threatening encounters with poisonous snakes in his stories. In a moment of inattention or carelessness, the character of the story would trespass into the danger zone and trigger the attack.

Striking with destructive intent, the snake would bury its fangs deep into human flesh. Compressing its jaws as it pumped poison into the wound, it would then release its victim to suffer the effect. With the poison came pain and the knowledge that swift action had to be taken if the victim was to live. Treatment of the bite and removal of the poison became *the* immediate priority of the person who had been bitten. Sin is a poison similar to snake venom except that it is a heart-based, social poison that destroys the relationships we were made for. We are not designed to live with sin any more than we were designed to live with snake venom flowing in our veins.

Sin causes spiritual, emotional, and even physical pain while robbing us of our ability to trust. It makes us feel alone and unlovable, and awakens in us the anger that is behind so many of the grudges we live with. Sin destroys intimacy and brings a burden of guilt that we cannot get rid of on our own and, when not dealt with, destroys our ability to have the kind of life-giving relationships we were created for. The question we face is what to do about the sin that is poisoning our lives. We can try to hide it, or ignore it, but refusing to deal with our sin will not fix the pain it causes, just as pretending nothing happened will not reverse the destructive effect of the venom coursing through the veins of a snakebite victim. The poison has to be dealt with and we cannot minimize it if we want to be free of its effect on our lives.

Though many people understand "sin" to mean the things we do that break God's commandments, there is more to it than outward actions, just as there is more to a weed than its flower. Sin, like weeds, has a root and, just as mowing weeds will not get rid of them, struggling with the symptoms of sin without addressing the root of the behavior will not affect real change either. Awareness of sin is the first step to gaining our freedom from it (Romans 5:20). As my friend Dale experienced in the previous chapter, embracing forgiveness requires getting honest about the sin that has been done. Like an addict who has to admit his sin of addiction, or an abuser who has to face the reality of what he has done if there is to be healing, we all have to come to a point of honesty regarding our sins if we are going to be able to take positive action. Just as sin is the poison that destroys, forgiveness is the antidote that heals.

What is sin?

Spiritual self-reliance is sin in its most basic form. Paul says that "whatever is not from faith is sin", meaning that trust in God is the foundation for a life free of sin's effects (Romans 14:23).

The Bible says that sin entered the human experience when the devil came to Adam and Eve with the temptation to take their lives into their own hands rather than continuing to trust God's leading and care. Gesturing to some of the fruit from the tree of the knowledge of good and evil, Satan basically said to them, "Bite this and you can be your own god. You can live your own life your own way by your own strength for your own purposes." Not fully realizing that it meant abandoning trust in God, the moment Adam and Eve took the devil up on his offer they discovered that saying "yes" to sin brought with it a world of self-centeredness and hurtful consequences (Genesis 3:5).

We were designed to live dependent on God. The Greek word, *hamartano*, translated "sin," literally means "to err" or to "miss the mark" and has to do with choosing to live outside of the way God designed us. That is the choice Adam and Eve made when they ate from the tree. They sank teeth into the fruit offered to them and, in doing so, gained personal experience of both good *and* evil. It altered how they viewed their world and interacted with each other (Genesis 2:17). Satan repeatedly uses the same strategy today that he used on Adam and Eve, tempting us to live life our way and without God. He knows that if he can get us to do it, he will have power to do his damage in our lives just as he did in theirs.

Everyone is affected by sin

The Bible teaches that sin went viral the instant it entered the human experience. Beginning with the first parents of humanity, sin spread to all who came after them and with it came spiritual death. It is in this sense that we can say we have inherited the sin of our forefathers.

"Therefore, just as through one man sin entered into the world, and death through sin, and so death spread to all men, because all sinned—for until the Law sin was in the world, but sin is not imputed when there is no law. Nevertheless death reigned from Adam until Moses, even over those who had not sinned in the likeness of the offense of Adam, who is a type of Him who was to come."

Romans 5:12-14

Through inherited sin came the seeds of self-centeredness (Psalm 51:5). That means that, regardless of age or ability, sin is first an attitude thing before it is a performance thing, existing in our hearts before we ever get a chance to act it out. There is no one day when we commit our first sin and lose our innocence because sin affects us from the moment of conception on. According to the Apostle Paul, we were born spiritually dead, rather than spiritually bad, and that deadness affects the way we relate to others, because we all carry and express inherent selfishness. Put succinctly, it means we were born cute rather than innocent.

Born self-centered

With sin came a sense of what was lost. Many of us understand what significant loss is like. We may have experienced the death of a loved one, left family and friends behind as we moved from one country to another, or lost valued relationships to betrayal. In whatever way it happened, the loss we have suffered will often have cost us our sense of belonging as well. Sin did this when it stripped the human race of its ability to belong to the family of God by shattering our core relationship with our Creator. From that moment, spiritual orphanhood spread to all people, bringing with it a sense of emptiness akin to what a newly orphaned child might experience after having lost his family (Romans 5:12-14).

Users

Lost identity and spiritual orphanhood changes the way we relate to others, driving us into a survival based mode of living with no one to depend on but ourselves. The more acutely we live with this sense of lostness the more it can drive us to the point of using others selfishly in our struggle to get our own needs met. It is this selfishness that thwarts our ability to have truly healthy relationships. The more selfish we become, the more self-centered actions become the norm as our sinful attitudes determine how we relate to those around us. Even when we do something outwardly nice for someone, if our actions are driven by the ulterior motive of doing it in order to get something back, sin is being expressed in the motive behind the act. It is this selfishness that can make us into what a friend of mine once graphically described as "users."

A "user" uses everyone around him for his own purposes, including God, himself, and others. He may try to use God by reworking his concept of God to make God someone who serves and blesses him rather than someone to be served and blessed *by* him. Often the only time a user talks to God is when he wants to use God to fix what is wrong in his life or when he wants God to bless his agenda. When there is pain, a user wants God to take it away so he can continue to follow his own desires rather than taking the trouble to change the behavior behind his pain. Often when God will not do what a user wants, the user gets angry or gives up on God.

A user even uses himself by simply making his life all about his own wants and desires. He uses his own strength, resources, and skills to meet his own needs and wants. Rather than giving himself to the service of God, a user serves his own self-interests with all the resources that he can lay his hands on.

A user also uses those around her. She will twist, pervert, and destroy her relationships simply by making them primarily about getting her own needs met first. To that end, she will often use others selfishly even if that purpose is only to fulfill her need to have someone to love so that she no longer has to feel alone. Like a mother who over-controls her child in the name of loving him while really holding on because she cannot bear to let him grow up, or a person who easily moves from friendship to friendship while she plays at being a friend so she can feel accepted, sometimes her selfishness does not look selfish on the surface, but to the degree that it is based on having her needs met first, it is phony at its core. Stained by self-centeredness, even the way she tries to love becomes an expression of her sin. As her need grows, she becomes grasping and, as she becomes grasping, her selfishness takes over and begins to direct the way she relates to others. Soon both God and people become important to her only to the degree that they can give her something. The tragic thing is that she can neither help it nor control it. She has to get her own needs met first.

Jesus taught that our actions come out of the attitudes within us (Matthew 15:19). As selfish attitudes motivate our actions, they wreak havoc in our relationships by driving us to do the things we do to one another. A man who is filled with anger on the inside tends to work that anger out on those around him through the way that he treats them. A woman who gossips maliciously about someone she once had as a friend sins in her heart against that friend before the words ever leave her mouth. A man who commits adultery first betrays his marriage by lusting after the other woman in his heart before actually doing the physical deed (Matthew 5:28). It is the heart that finds expression in the action and, no matter how much we might struggle to change how we act on the outside, our inner motivations will continue to drive our outer actions until we experience a change of heart.

Only the power of God can change the heart and, until that happens, our efforts to eradicate the effects of sin in our lives will prove futile. A friend once compared controlling sin to trying to nail gelatin to a wall. It cannot be done. Assuming I could hold it in place long enough to get a nail through it, it would ooze off the nail and run down the wall, resisting my attempts to make it do what I wanted it to do. In the same way, the Apostle Paul says sin powerfully resists our attempts to control it as it fights in us against everything we know to be right and healthy. If left to our own resources, we will be helpless against its power and ultimately fall into a deep despair brought on by our inability to defeat the relational poison we call "sin." But there is help to be had. God has not left us to deal with sin on our own (Romans 7:21 – 8:1).

Facing the reality

Biblically speaking, there are two ways we can deal with our sin. The first is to get honest with God and let Him forgive us. The second usually involves some sort of cover-up as we try to hide what we have done (1 John 1:9; John 3:20). Our motives for doing so can range from hoping that if we can keep what we have done hidden we might be able to get away with it (sometimes even going so far as to redefine what we have done so we do not have to admit that it is sin), to simply avoiding the discomfort of having to confront the consequences of our actions. Unfortunately, in the same way that a patient has to confront a medical issue diagnosed by his doctor, there is no way to deal with sin without directly confronting the reality of it. The day my father was diagnosed with cancer, his doctor explained the gravity of his situation clearly so he could take immediate action on choosing a program of treatment. Like a doctor who is candid with his patient so that he can get on with the treatment of a life-threatening disease, God sometimes has to show us our sin so graphically that we are finally driven to the necessary action of dealing with it (Romans 5:20).

God has come searching for us in order to restore us to the freedom from sin that we were designed to live in. Gaining that freedom means admitting that we are helpless to free ourselves by our own strength. In the moment of getting real and saying "yes" to Christ, the Spirit of God gives us insight, conviction, and the strength needed to make the necessary choices. According to Paul, in that moment, we begin to live by God's strength rather than our own. Making this choice will often mean the beginning of a whole new adventure of faith as God begins to guide our living (Galatians 5:16).

Accepting our freedom can sometimes mean more than just walking away from a situation. There are times that God will ask us to make amends with those we have wronged as a way of expressing His love and blessing to those whom we have hurt. When this happens, it is never to be seen as punishment for what we have done, but only as a way of sharing the blessing we have already received in the forgiveness God has given us. If we fail to recognize that we are bringing a blessing and see ourselves as having to pay for what we have done, we will miss our freedom. God does not forgive us and then demand that we pay for our sin. God forgives us and then uses us to bless those around us, including those who were once our enemies.

Like an addict who finally admits he is helpless in the face of his addiction, we too must come to the point that we are ready for the kind of help that can only come from a totally non-self-centered source – God Himself (John 3:16). Sin does not have to be the end for us. There is freedom to be had. Jesus brings us always back to one simple message: Repent and believe for the Kingdom of Heaven is at hand. Simply put, Jesus asks us to go into the darkness and call out His name. He promises to meet us there (Mark 1:15; John 1:4-5).

Questions:

• What new insight have you gained about sin?

• Has someone in your life sinned against you? If so, how does the idea that sin drives what people do affect the way you see what they have done to you?

• God needs to show us our sin so we can give it to Him. What does the idea say to you? Have you experienced this? What was the result?

Chapter 8

The Process of Surrender

When it comes to broken relationships, making the choice to affirm unhealthy behavior is akin to sticking our head in the sand. No matter how well intentioned we are, affirmation that fails to deal with the sin that is destroying a person's life is as ineffective as telling an abuse victim to pretend that nothing really happened. It is another form of denial and helps no one. We cannot just tell someone who is struggling with a broken relationship that they are a good person and make everything okay. The pain and trauma done to us through sin and betrayal cannot just be thrown aside. It needs to be healed and that healing is at the core of Jesus' call to repent and believe.

A new way of living

"The time is fulfilled, and the kingdom of God is at hand; repent and believe in the gospel."

Mark 1:15

The call to repent and believe is a call to change our approach to life, including the way we deal with the pain and anger of betrayal and failed relationships. The most important thing that we can bring to God in response to His call is a willingness to change. He will do the rest. The deeper our surrender to God, the deeper our freedom will be.

A number of years ago, I was teaching in a university setting and had chosen "repentance" as my topic. Shortly after my session ended, I was approached by an older female student who seemed quite agitated. She acted as though she did not know quite how to approach the subject but her struggle with the material was enough to make her overcome her natural reticence and confront the issue directly. "I don't like that word," she blurted out. "What word?" I asked her. "That word 'repent.'

I've heard it all my life and I'm tired of beating myself up every time I fail. I'd rather affirm people and tell them that God loves them than threaten them with punishment."

It seemed she heard the gospel of Mark in a different way than I had and I could hear her performance-based background coming out as she talked. She understood repentance not in terms of surrender to God's grace, but in terms of punishment for her failure to perform correctly, and wanted to replace what she saw as an oppressive teaching with a more "positive" focus. For her, punishment and repentance were synonymous – an archaic concept she thought best dispensed with – and so she determined to try to love people through simply affirming them in whatever way she could. I resonated a bit with what she was trying to do as I had had my own struggle with a legalistic approach to following God, but I was also hesitant to simply discard Jesus' teaching just because it was difficult.

Repentance, belief, and the benefit of sin

Repentance means changing direction and involves renouncing what we get from our old way of handling relationships. We must understand who we are putting our faith in and actively make the choice to trust Him. Christ's call to repent and believe begins with an honest confession of our sin and a renunciation of the benefits we get from it. Having confessed and renounced the old, sinful, and selfish ways of handling our betrayers, we are called to trust Jesus, as He leads us in a new way of dealing with what has been done to us. This allows Christ to pour His Spirit into our lives and bring His strength to bear where ours has not been adequate.

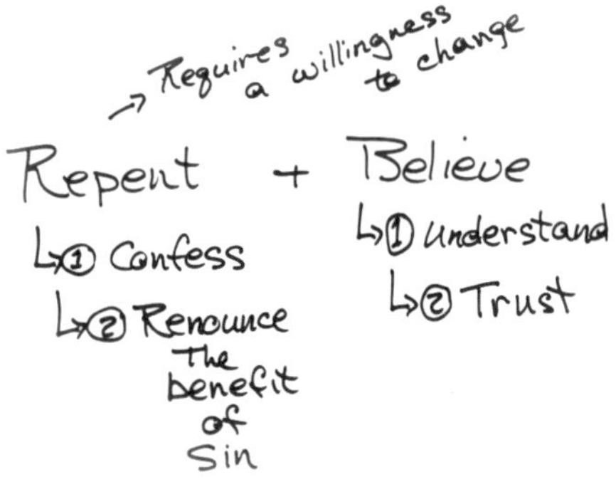

Responding to the call to repent and believe requires a willingness to embrace change. Mouthing the words of a confession alone does not make people free because not everyone who confesses is ready for the kind of change that true repentance brings. A mentor of mine used to say that, in order to become free, a person had to be *willing* to be free. I had always assumed that anyone struggling with the brokenness that sin causes would be willing to be free, but I found out that it was not always the case.

We are often slow about giving up sinful activity because it generates a benefit that we like. The devil understands the concept of attaching a benefit, or "enticement," to a sin and he does it regularly. He enticed Adam and Eve in the Garden with the promise that they could become like God. Liking the sound of that, they bit the forbidden fruit and humanity struggles with the consequence of their actions to this day. The "benefit" strategy is one of the devil's most effective ways of getting us to continue to trade our freedom for some minimal benefit that we have decided we cannot do without.

The idea that his sins had a benefit was a new one for Stanley.

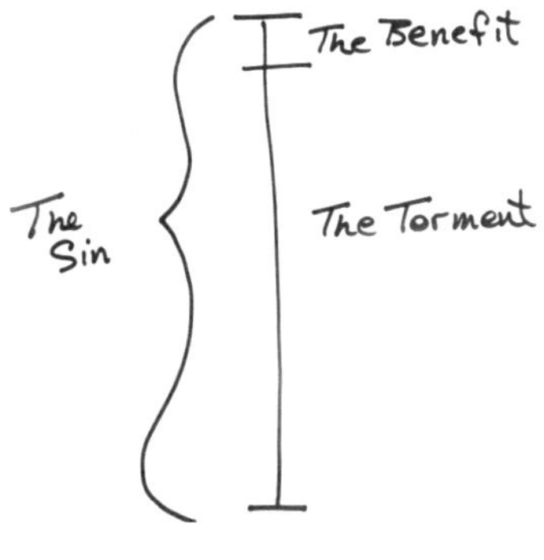

Stanley was an alcoholic. In the pursuit of his addiction, he had betrayed everyone who loved him and himself as well. He spoke of the pain his addiction had caused him and how he just wanted to be done with it. I could hear his despair over the fact that no matter how much he confessed it, the sin he struggled with just would not go away. Guilt and anger were his everyday companions and, in order to deal with his pain, he took the only approach he knew by drinking more than ever. When he asked if I could help him, I asked him what he loved so much about his sin.

Stanley sat silent as he processed the question. When he finally responded, he said, "I've never really thought of it that way." In preparation for the next time we would meet, I asked him to take some time and be deliberate about thinking it through, and then make a list of what he got from his sin and why he enjoyed it so much. We ended our time together and he went off to do his homework.

At our next meeting, Stanley was slow to speak and sat quietly in his chair. Making a list of the benefits of his sin had been an eye-opener for him. He had begun to see how much he got from his addiction and how it had become his coping mechanism. When life became more than he could deal with, alcohol gave him a way out. Booze was his escape and that escape was his benefit. The question he had to ask himself was if he was really ready to give up his old way of dealing with his stress. If so, he would have to develop new and healthier ways of handling what life threw at him, though it would take some work. It would also take a degree of trust in God that was beyond his current understanding of what it meant to live by faith. Stanley looked at the trade-off he would have to make and came to the conclusion that he was not at all sure that he was ready to make that choice.

Pain reduction and willingness to change

When it comes right down to it, many of us do not really want change. What we want is pain reduction. We just want someone to take the pain away and let us go on doing what we have become accustomed to doing. How many times have we prayed that God take the pain away so that we could go on living the way we want, failing to understand that our unhealthy behavior is what is causing the pain in the first place? Stanley was like that. He wanted his alcohol and the escape it brought. He just did not want all the negative side effects that his drinking produced. Once he came to realize that he could not have it both ways, he was faced with a choice. He could keep the behavior and the pain that went with it, or he could renounce the benefit of his behavior and begin the journey to freedom. One way or the other, the behavior had to go if he was to truly gain the freedom to change his life.

Repenting means more than just saying we are sorry. However we look at it, in order to gain our freedom, we have to be willing to give something up. For the person who loves to hate the one who hurt her, true repentance may mean having to give up the delicious sense of vengeance she gets from gossiping about that person. For the one who has had something valuable stolen, it might mean having to give up his demand for compensation. For the person who has been betrayed, it could mean having to release her betrayer into the hands of God along with her demands for justice. In the case of the addict, it might mean having to give up the escape that his addiction brings him. He must make the choice to deal with life and relationships without the comfort of his booze or drugs.

Unwillingness to give up the benefit of sin is the reason that many never receive measurable freedom. I have come to realize that we cannot pray the pain away without embracing change, yet I have repeatedly encountered people unwilling to give up some behavior that caused them pain. Why? Because they wanted to keep what the behavior got them. Invariably, such people walk away frustrated. That said, I have also had the privilege of working with those who concluded that their sin was no longer worth the pain it was causing. As they engaged Jesus' call to repentance and belief *out of a willingness to be done with the benefit of their sin*, they gained their freedom. It is the willingness to change that is crucial in repentance and belief because it allows God to do what He came to do. It does not take much. I have often seen God work with very little as He sought to bring someone into the freedom He designed them for. Marcy was one such person.

"Just to see what would happen"– Marcy's story

Marcy was a rape survivor. The violence that had been done to her had stripped her of her quality of life and left her mired in bitterness and rage. She came to a Forgiveness Seminar looking for a way to deal with the anger that was poisoning her life. It was the teaching on repentance and belief that impacted her the most strongly. Fascinated by the thought that her sin carried a benefit, she was specifically struck by the statement that she needed to be willing to renounce that benefit and take the step of trusting Jesus with the way she had been wronged.

Marcy approached me during a break. "I know what my benefit is." She spoke very deliberately. "I love hating my perpetrator." She went on to describe the night of her abuse and how, for her, justice had never been done. "I live in fear of him. I hate him and I like hating him." Like many victims who feel powerless to deal with what has been done to them, she had developed her own way of dealing with her sense of helplessness and violation. She nursed her hatred and enacted her vengeance through a ritualistic fantasy life that she indulged in regularly. Finding a place where she could be alone, she would close her eyes and call up the memory of that night. As she replayed the event in her mind's eye, the rage would flood through her body, bringing with it a rush of hormones very much like a drug-induced "high." Indeed, she had become addicted to this sensation. "And then," she said, "I kill him." She went on to describe her violent imaginations in some detail; "It's the only way I can work out my anger. I love it. That's my benefit."

I decided on a direct approach largely because I had no idea how to gently respond to what she had just told me. "Are you willing to forgive him?" I asked. She stared back at me with angry eyes and bluntly stated, "No. I am not."

I wondered how firm her 'no' was and so I phrased my next question this way: "Would you be willing to invite Jesus into the situation?" She stared at me silently for a moment as she weighed what I had said. When she spoke, her words carried an edge. "Maybe. Just to see what would happen." Not knowing exactly what Jesus would do with this little opening in her armor of hatred, I responded, "Okay, pray with me," and I helped her to pray a prayer inviting Jesus into the situation "just to see what would happen."

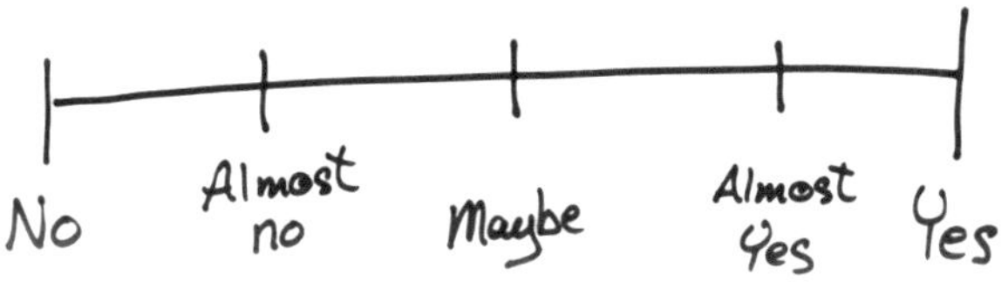

When Marcy said "no" to my initial question about her willingness to forgive her perpetrator, I wanted to find out if her response was an absolute one or not. I grew up believing that "yes" was "yes" and "no" was "no," but have since come to realize that people are not always so black and white in their decision-making and desires. There can be a "mostly yes," a "maybe" and a "mostly no" as well. You cannot really help someone whose "no" is absolute, but, for someone whose "no" is not absolute, there can be opportunity for the Spirit of Christ to do what He does best. When Marcy responded to my next question with, "Maybe. Just to see what will happen," I knew that we had some room to work. It was into that little bit of willingness that we invited Jesus to do what He wanted to do in her life. Helping her to pray was all that remained.

Helping people pray

Marcy did not know how to pray what needed to be prayed. Often, people in situations like Marcy's struggle with ineffectual prayers as they call out to God, wondering why they seem to get no answer. It could be that they are praying unrealistic prayers, or selfish prayers, but sometimes it is just a case of needing some help in framing a prayer that honestly and directly says what they need to express. I listened carefully to what Marcy had to say and, as she voiced her willingness to pray with me that evening, we took time to express back to Jesus the contents of our discussion. She stared with angry eyes at the back of the chair in front of her as we framed the prayer around what she had told me: "Dear Jesus, I come to You to put my abuser into your hands. I hate him. I love hating him and I'm not willing to forgive him. I even love killing him every night in my mind."

Marcy broke off and turned toward me. "We can pray that?"

I responded, "You're just being honest. God sees it in your heart anyway." She went back to staring at the chair in front of her and we continued, "Dear Jesus, I love killing him in my mind and I'm not willing to stop doing that. But I'm willing to invite You into this situation just to see what will happen. Amen."

Though I know that Jesus will often work powerfully when invited into a situation, I rarely know what exactly He will do. During that very raw prayer time, Jesus took Marcy at the place she could meet Him and intervened on her behalf.

The next day, Marcy approached me directly, "After we prayed last night, I went home and tested the prayer." Wondering to myself how you "test" that kind of prayer, I listened as she described how she had gone home and prepared for her evening ritual. Once settled, she had closed her eyes and called the memory to mind, ready for the flush of rage to come as it usually did. "I couldn't make it happen," she said. "I couldn't make the rage come. No matter how many times I did it I couldn't get angry." Marcy looked at me with questioning eyes and asked, "What happened?"

We both knew that somehow God had touched her and that knowledge made her ready for more. The obvious intervention of the Spirit of God in her life brought with it a renewed sense of hope, something long dead in Marcy's life. That little bit of hope was all Marcy needed to jolt her out of her destructive routine and make her ready to begin the journey to wholeness. I was amazed at how the Spirit of God could do so much with so little and I marveled at how, overnight, He had moved her from one end of the willingness spectrum to the other and set her on the road to wholeness.

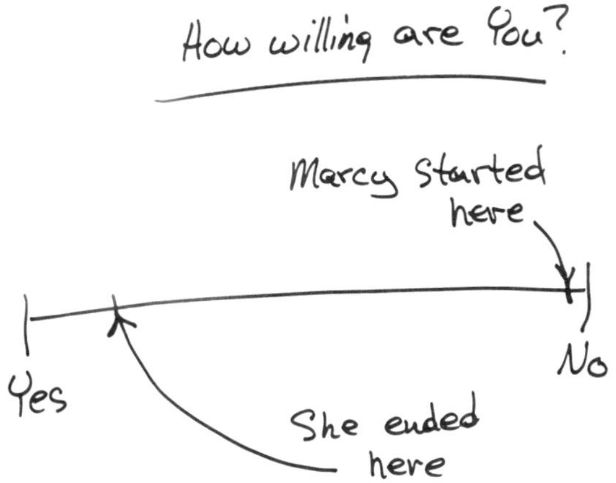

Marcy was a church-attending Christian who had been living with the paralyzing effects of unforgiveness. She could not remember the last time she had felt God's presence, because her unforgiveness had blocked her from experiencing His closeness. Having begun her journey into healing that day, she went on with some help to engage a lifestyle of forgiveness. As she offered her little bit of willingness to Jesus, He empowered her to get honest in confessing her sin bluntly, renouncing the benefits of her sin of hatred, and inviting Him into the place where it ruled her life. As she engaged the process of repentance and belief, Marcy discovered that what began as a moment must grow into a lifestyle. What had happened during the prayer we prayed together needed to be followed up with ongoing action if the freedom was to deepen and become her new reality.

For Marcy, an initial forgiveness event became the beginning of a whole new way of living. Although she had experienced an amazing breakthrough at a forgiveness seminar, much more lay ahead of her. As the newness of her experience wore off, she began to realize that it would be easy to go back to using her old methods of coping with the injustice of her situation. Temptations did come and she was faced with making a choice to handle things differently. Remembering that repentance means to "choose another way," Marcy began to implement what she had learned. Each time she felt the temptation to slip back into the old ways, she would take time to sit before God and place her antagonist in His hands. As she renounced the benefit of her old sin, she discovered that God was near to her, drawing her forward through the pain and anger to a place of healing.

Marcy soon realized that this was only the beginning of something much deeper than she could have imagined at the time. Memories of other betrayals began to resurface. As she became aware that she still lived with the aftermath of other pains from her past, she began the process of placing the memories of these old hurts and betrayals into the hands of Jesus. This new approach to handling pain and anger brought real change to her as she became increasingly honest with herself, with God, and with others. She no longer suffered in silence and isolation, but took the initiative to ask people she had come to trust to pray with her. Step by step the old cycle of unforgiveness began to fall away and she began to walk in new freedom. Marcy had hit the bottom of her barrel at the conference that night and became ready to embrace the change that lay ahead.

The bottom of the barrel

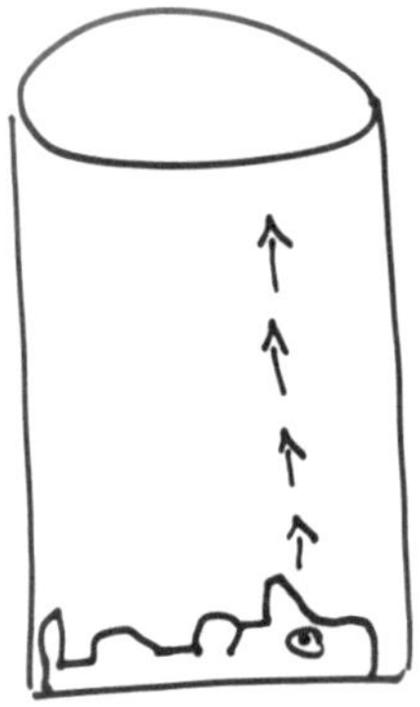

Change does not come easy and, on top of that, many of us do not really know how to change. That said, change is necessary for growth to happen. My Grandpa once compared the difficulty of making lasting change to falling into a barrel. He said that nobody was really willing to change until they hit bottom and went on to describe the bottom of the barrel as a place of helplessness where there is nothing left to fight. He said coming to that point is not easy but it is crucial because it shifts our focus from battling our situation to surrendering to the Savior. As he talked, I pictured myself falling down the inside of an old wooden barrel, fighting and clawing at the sides in a futile attempt to stop my plunge. Once I hit bottom, everything changed. I was no longer staring down at my situation but was now looking up to where help would come from.

When we hit bottom, we finally become willing to both receive and give what the Bible calls mercy. It is like a drowning person who looks up in the midst of his inability to save himself and sees his rescuer. Ready to be rescued, and eager to put his faith in someone else's strength and ability, he is finally able to trust another person with his situation. For someone struggling with guilt, anger, or betrayal, Jesus' teaching on repentance and belief is the key to receiving the mercy we need. It is a call to turn from our way to God's way and, in the process, to surrender our struggle as we exchange our old, ineffective ways of dealing with our pain and anger for a new way empowered by God Himself.

The call to repent and believe becomes most real in time of need as it leads us to abandon ourselves into the hands of God. It also requires a willingness to surrender our agenda and trust Him with whatever the future might hold. When we engage the call to repent and believe, we give God access to our broken relationships so that He can do what he came to do – rescue us from the relationship-destroying power of sin.

Questions:

• How does the idea that sin has benefits affect you?

• Do you have any relationships in which you see a need for change? What is causing you to resist making the change you need to make?

• What will it take to make you willing to change?

Chapter 9

Forgiveness-based Living

Why can't I just do it once?

"Why do I have to repent over and over? Doesn't it 'take' the first time?" The question was brought to me by a young man during the afternoon break at a forgiveness seminar and I could hear the frustration in his voice as he asked it. Ethan had just learned that forgiveness begins with a one-time event but also involves coming to God on a regular basis. He was frustrated with the idea that he could not just do it once and get on with life. The idea of regular repentance seemed to suggest that somehow God's forgiveness wore off as time went on and he wanted a magic moment that would fix life permanently. He demanded to know why it could not be that way.

Embracing a forgiveness lifestyle involves both maintaining and deepening our relationships with God and others. It takes work and, as the relationships move forward, our tendency will be to return to the old, selfish ways that we have been accustomed to because they are what we know. Many people experience forgiveness and yet gradually lose their sense of peace, falling back into bitterness again as time passes and the freshness of the "forgiveness event" wears off. Is God somehow unfaithful? Is His grace a temporary thing? Several biblical passages address the problem of a fading sense of God's grace and our tendency to drift back to our old ways (Galatians 1:6; 3:3; 2 Peter 1:9).

Whether it is with God, a friend, or a spouse, any close relationship will bring an opportunity for us to give and receive forgiveness on a regular basis because it is a part of the process of growing together. On our wedding day, my fiancée and I stood at the altar and said "yes." In that moment we got all there was to get of each other. I have since questioned whether we really knew all that we got. The short response is "No, we didn't." Since then, our marriage has become a process of getting to know each other more deeply.

Time and again we have offended or hurt one another. We have had to forgive repeatedly but, over the years, our commitment to forgive when necessary has developed a deep freedom within our relationship. It is the freedom of knowing that the forgiveness will not end and that we *will* be loved regardless of the mistakes we make. This kind of freedom is the foundation of all enduring relationships. It carries with it the understanding that although a forgiveness-based lifestyle begins with a single event it develops into something we continue to do because we know it is the healthiest way to live.

Christ calls us to relationships based on more than sporadic visits with God driven by our need for relief from guilt. The choice to adopt a lifestyle of ongoing forgiveness is a deliberate one and helps to prevent the accumulation of unhealthy anger and bitterness. It can be compared to the way in which taking out the trash regularly prevents a home from becoming a toxic environment for those who live there. Disposing of the trash was one of the chores we children got to do every time we went to visit Grandpa and Grandma at the farm. Garbage was never allowed to stack up around the farmhouse because it stank and made life unpleasant. As fast as it accumulated it was taken to the burn pit and incinerated. In a like manner, Jesus wants to deal with our garbage *as it happens*. Unless we allow Him to do so, we will end up living lives ridden by guilt, punctuated by fleeting moments of relief as we visit God's grace – and this only when we can no longer deal with the accumulation of shame on our own. Jesus told His disciples to live with Him full time. Condemnation and guilt do not accumulate in our lives when we live "in" Christ because His Spirit deals with our garbage on a daily basis (John 15:4; Romans 8:1).

So, how often do we have to forgive? Often, Christ taught that if our brother sins, rebuke him, and, if he repents, forgive him; and, if he sins seven times a day and comes back and repents, forgive him again (Luke 17:3-5). With Jesus, there really is no end to forgiveness. His only requirement is the willingness to give Him what we carry and to live in His presence. When we live in Christ, exposed to His love for us on a regular basis, the conviction grows in us that, no matter how great the stumbling, God's grace is greater still (Romans 5:20). We increasingly come to live without condemnation and guilt, not because we have done nothing wrong, but because we regularly give to Christ all that would steal our sense of freedom.

In any relationship, there are easy days and hard days. On the hard days, we will be called to face what has happened, either to apologize or to grant forgiveness, often having to do both. Being aware of this helps us become deliberate in developing the discipline of forgiving. By resolving matters quickly, we protect our relationships by preventing unresolved bitterness from building up. Meanwhile, our intimacy with each other grows due to the knowledge that, regardless of our failure, we will still be loved. It is the same in our walk with God as it is with our other relationships. Just as young marrieds do not fully understand the depth of the commitment they are making on their wedding day, we do not fully know what we are getting into the day we say "yes" to the life Christ calls us to. Yet God walks with us as our relationships deepen and unfold, repeatedly demonstrating His faithfulness and love as He gives us the grace we need in the situations where we need it.

Becoming proactive

Adopting a forgiveness lifestyle means exchanging a reactive approach to relationships for a proactive one.

We learn to interact proactively with others based on what we know to be healthy rather than reacting out of how we feel.

One Sunday, as I prepared for morning worship in the Church where

I was the pastor, Melvin approached me in the foyer. By the set of his jaw and the look in his eyes, I could tell he was on a mission. He was angry and what he had to say reflected the offenses that he had allowed to build up within himself. "Pastor," he said, "I am leaving this Church. I just wanted to tell you before I did it." Setting aside my initial reaction to the harshness of his approach, I asked him why he had made his choice to leave. "I'm not getting what I need here," he responded. Before I could stop myself, the words came out of my mouth: "I think God wants you to grow up."

Did I just say that!?

Both of us were dumbfounded at my lack of tact and pastoral sensitivity. It was an awkward moment. My response was not the one Melvin had expected and I admired the way he rallied to overcome his momentary shock. As he struggled to formulate his reply, I quietly asked him what he meant when he said he was not getting what he needed. He shared his sense of not belonging, describing the people at Church as unfriendly and unaccepting, and said he was tired of trying to fit into a community that did not care enough to want him.

I asked Melvin to elaborate and he spoke of how Sunday after Sunday he had come to Church, waiting for someone to approach him to start a conversation, only nobody did. As he watched the people visit with each other, he began to take offense and, as the offenses accumulated, he obsessed over them. In his mind, the people were uncaring and unloving, and he began to see himself as the victim of their selfishness. Soon he had had enough. It was time to leave but he could not do so without saying something first. His need to voice his offense led him to me that Sunday morning so that he could deliver his parting shot and then depart, feeling justified in doing so.

I was struck by the reactivity of his approach to the Church community and asked him to stick with me for a six-week experiment, saying that he could leave with my blessing if the experiment failed. I told Melvin I wanted him to make a deliberate shift in the way he interacted with others when he came to Church. His task was to find two people each Sunday whom he could bless. Rather than waiting for someone to approach him with a greeting, he would choose someone and approach them. The change I was suggesting was simple and yet profound because it targeted Melvin's motives for coming to worship and moved him from a paradigm of selfishness to one of selflessness. It set the stage for him to come to Church for what he could give rather than for what he wanted to get.

At the end of six weeks, I asked him how things were going. "Oh, Pastor, things are so different now!" he exclaimed. As he spoke, he glowed with satisfaction over what he was experiencing. He had learned to make it his main priority to be a blessing to others rather than demanding that they serve his needs first. His new proactive approach had changed his view of how to be a part of a healthy faith community and had given him a sense of what Jesus meant when He told His disciples, "My food is to do the will of Him who sent Me" (John 4:34).

Jesus' teaching on repentance and belief is a proactive approach to changing not only the way we deal with past hurts but also the way that we will deal with the hurts yet to come. By forgiving and adopting a selfless rather than a selfish approach to others, we spend less time coping and more time living in freedom, less time living as "victims" and more time in the victory Christ has won over our situation. Living this way requires being deliberate about growing in maturity as it is often much easier to sulk and suffer than it is to proactively forgive. Fueled by anger and self-pity, the "sulk and suffer" stage can feel good, and our sense of being offended will lead us there if we are not careful. However, learning to say "no" to that temptation and choosing to forgive proactively will make us less selfish and more able to experience the joy and freedom we were designed for.

As Melvin made the shift toward serving others rather than demanding they serve him, it allowed him to let go of his offenses and to feel that he belonged. Somewhere in the process of repenting of his old approach to Church, Melvin entrusted to God the offenses he had built up, both imagined and real. As the joy that forgiveness brings replaced the bitterness, his ability to be a healthy part of her community was restored.

Questions:

• Do you have any relationships in which you need to become more proactive and less reactive? Which ones?

• Would you generally describe yourself as a proactive person or a reactive person when it comes to your relationships? How can you be more proactive?

• Repentance and belief is a process as well as an event. In what way does seeing this impact the way you deal with broken relationships?

Chapter 10

The Danger of Deceit

Silence can be a form of deceit

Relationships thrive when they are based on honesty and faithfulness but break down when we lie to one another. Deceit is a form of betrayal that prevents the formation of healthy, intimate relationships by destroying the trust that those relationships are built on. We can deceive one another either actively or passively, meaning we can either openly lie to one another or we can deceive by pretending that everything is fine when it is not. Some of us have used silence as a way of coping with conflict for so long that we do not even see it as a form of deceit, but it is. Without fully recognizing what we are doing, we manipulate our situations out of what we think are good intentions, often telling ourselves that we are just trying to protect those whom we love. We are called avoiders.

Vince's story

Vince was an avoider. Vince was also a crack addict, was married, and had a family. A crack addict with a family who did not like to be up front with his problems. It was a recipe for disaster that often repeated itself.

Vince had a cycle that he lived over and over. He would be clean for a while and then his addictive tendencies would begin to make themselves felt. Beginning with one cigarette a day, he would start smoking again, quickly graduating to a pack a day. Following that came alcohol, beginning with the need to buy one beer and moving swiftly into binge drinking. From there, it was only a short matter of time until he was overcome by a driving need to buy crack cocaine. Then the whole thing accelerated until he would wake up in jail, having once again destroyed his family's hopes and livelihood. Vince would then pick up the shattered remnants of his life to try to rebuild something of normalcy and the cycle would begin again.

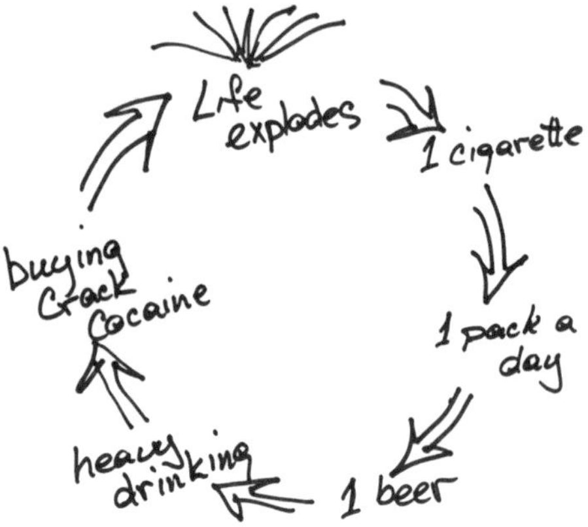

Vince came looking for help. As he told me his story, he said, "My kids hate me. I don't know about my wife. I've hurt her so much."

I asked him, "Where are you at in your cycle?" A haunted look came into his eyes, "I've started smoking again. I'm up to three cigarettes a day."

I asked him if he had told his wife. "I can't do that to her!" Vince spoke in an anguished tone, "Not again!"

But Vince *was* doing it to her again. By keeping silent about his struggle, he guaranteed that she would not be able to help him until it was too late and their lives imploded yet one more time. His silence was actually setting her up for more pain than if he would just take the risk to tell her what was going on. How could I explain it? Ah! An image came to mind. Taking a piece of paper, I began to draw.

"Vince," I said, "this graph shows time on the bottom. The farther we go along the line, the more time has gone by. The vertical line shows the level of pain. The higher we go up the line, the more pain we are talking about." I drew a diagonal line across the graph with a short vertical line near the beginning of the time line showing minimal time elapsed and a long vertical line farther along indicating a longer time lapse. "This is the choice you need to make. The sooner you get honest, the less pain you'll cause. The longer you wait, the more pain you'll cause."

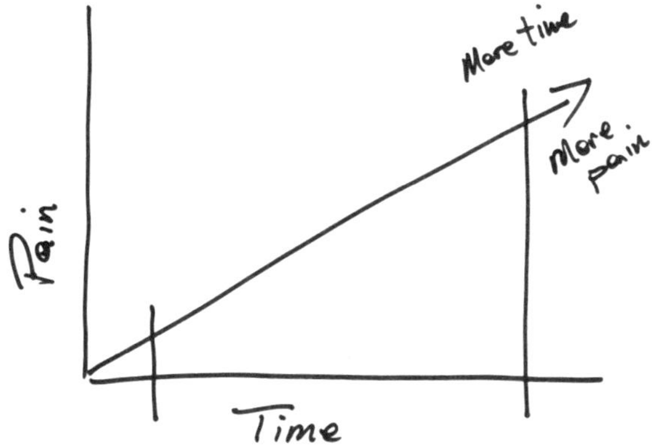

I saw understanding in Vince's eyes. He stared at my chart, weighing his options, and finally came to a decision. He could not do it. He left my office to fight his battle alone, trying to protect his loved ones by his silence while he fought his addiction on his own. A couple of weeks later he called me from jail. He had not come clean or allowed others to help. With another cycle complete, evil had wreaked its havoc in Vince's family one more time.

Get rid of the deceit

Fear of the consequences of honest communication – and how others might react to what we say – can make silence a tempting way to avoid the stress of having to face problems in our relationships. Keeping quiet about issues may seem like the easiest option, yet honesty is critical if we are going to deny the devil the opportunity he seeks to do his work.

Being truthful with each other allows us to stand together and help one another, even though the risk involved in sharing where we are at can be difficult. It can help to know that choosing silence actually sets us up for more trauma when the truth finally does come out, as it did with Vince. Sometimes overcoming the silence only happens when the pain, generated by our actions, gets so great that change becomes necessary.

I grew up with cartoon images of ostriches sticking their heads in the sand in order to hide from danger. With his head in the sand and his behind in the air, it was always clear that the ostrich was not effectively dealing with reality. While not a true representation of the way an actual ostrich handles danger in the wild, it is a great image of how many of us use avoidance as a way of dealing with conflict and offense. Healthy relationships require that we get real with one another while making the choice to speak about what has come between us. Though good communication skills do not usually come naturally and have to be learned, the effort is well worth it. Sharing honestly can feel dangerous and we may feel we are risking rejection if we choose to speak about what we are struggling with. That said, I have found that my family always gives me more grace than I give myself. This may not be the case in every family or friendship, but it *is* the case in those relationships where the love of Christ is foundational. We really do *want* to love one another.

Vince's story taught me that silent avoidance can be just as destructive to relationships as bold-faced lies. In Ephesians, the Apostle Paul calls us to deal openly and honestly with the issues that come up in our relationships until we have resolved them as far as is possible. He warns us that the devil can mess with us if we choose dishonesty as a way of relating to each other.

"...laying aside falsehood, speak truth each one of you with his neighbor, for we are members of one another. Be angry, and yet do not sin; do not let the sun go down on your anger, and do not give the devil an opportunity."

Ephesians 4:25-27

What can you do if you are a "Vince" who does not know how to come clean with those he loves? By taking seriously Jesus' call to repent and believe, you can turn from the old way and trust God to lead you in a new way of handling relationships. Andrea and Denis learned how to do this and it saved their marriage.

Andrea and Denis' story

Andrea and Denis overcame the silence and survived the affair. Learning to communicate openly and to leave the silence behind was crucial to the recovery of their relationship. Andrea tells her story this way:

"Until I finally opened up and told Denis everything he needed to know with complete openness and honesty, we were pretty much just spinning our tires in the mud. Until then, neither of us was able to actually move forward, and the broken trust between us remained shattered in a million pieces on the floor. But as I finally allowed him to see into the world of my affair – by giving the entire truth and nothing but the truth – those scattered shards of trust in our relationship began to ever so slowly start piecing back together.

Having face-to-face discussions on such difficult topics can be really tough to get through constructively. Along the way, we discovered a few helps that eased the whole process of coming clean. We'd heard of other couples who would only do phone conversations to talk about the affair, or wait to have their discussions in a more public setting (such as a coffee shop) to maintain a level of comfort and civility.

What eventually wound up working best for us was to answer questions over e-mail. Denis would send me a list of questions he wanted answers to, and then I would commit to answering them via e-mail within the next 48 hours. It worked really well (I wish we had known just to do this in the first place). I found that e-mail dialogue made it much easier for me to be totally honest because I didn't have to witness his initial reaction. It prevented my inclination to alter my responses out of fear or concern for the outcome. We also had a rule that he wasn't to read them until a time when he was alone, allowing for him to deal with his emotions in a way that didn't leave me having to bear the brunt of them.

Another thing I want to mention about openness and honesty is that the value of it doesn't lie solely in the confessions of the unfaithful spouse. Just as much value was gained when Dennis began to practice being more open and honest with me about what was going on for him. Our bond truly began to strengthen to the point where he (for the first time in our marriage) started opening up and sharing his own honest feelings, struggles, and fears. It drew us deeper into connection with one another when he finally allowed me the opportunity to understand him, care for him, and support him in ways I never knew to do before. My respect for him grew leaps and bounds, and I began to feel safe and more like a woman with him, as he truly allowed me to see his heart."

As they got honest with each other, Andrea and Denis allowed their anger to become a positive force that drove them to become real with one another. Once they had decided their relationship was worth more than could be gained by continuing on in the same old way, they made the choice to learn to communicate openly. They forgave and received forgiveness, both from each other and from God. In the end, a deeper intimacy was their reward. In the process, they learned about anger.

Be angry

We need to differentiate between two kinds of anger as we learn to be honest in our relationships. The first is fleshly anger. Essentially selfish and focused on hating the person who has hurt us, it is easiest to react out of this kind of anger. James calls it the "anger of man" and cautions us that, if we allow fleshly anger to dictate how we react, we will *not* end up with a healthy solution (James 1:19-20).

The second kind of anger is godly anger and it focuses on the sin that is harming the relationship rather than on hating the person who has hurt us. It is the kind of anger that motivated Jesus as He cleansed the temple, intent on removing the sin that was negatively affecting the people's worship of God while bringing the temple's focus back to what it should be (Matthew 21:12). Godly anger can be a powerful motivator in driving us to take the action necessary to do what is healthy for our relationships.

Relationships and anger go hand in hand. We all make each other angry at some point. Anger is an emotional response; it is not a sin in itself. The important thing is what we do with our anger. Paul tells us to be angry, just not to sin in our anger (Ephesians 4:26). Rather than allowing it to dictate how we respond, it *can* be used in a healthy way. Anger only becomes an unhealthy emotion when it takes over, clouding our ability to focus on the problem and filling us with hate for the other person rather than hate for the sin that has separated us. Paul warns that the devil can sometimes gain a measure of influence in the lives of those who allow anger to morph into hatred for another person.

Anger and communication must go hand in hand and, however we do it, we must talk with one another. Write a letter. Ask a counselor, a pastor, a friend, or a family member to sit in with you and the person you have an issue with as you get real with them (Matthew 18:15) . It may mean going for a coffee in a neutral, but private, place or using e-mail as a way of sharing openly with the other person. If you have to meet face to face, book time to do it so that your sharing is structured and the other party comes to the conversation already knowing that some issues are going to be discussed. Open the conversation by saying, "I have something difficult that I need to share with you..."and wait for them to indicate whether they are ready to hear you. If you have to, make notes or write a script for yourself so that, in the pressure of the moment, you do not forget what you want to say. Be honest and speak the truth in love (Ephesians 4:15), remembering that, by doing so, we deny the devil opportunity to do his damage in our lives and relationships. Silence is not an option if we want to live in the freedom that forgiveness brings.

But what if the devil has already found an opportunity and gained a foothold in our lives through unresolved anger and hatred? For those suffering in this way, forgiveness is still the only answer to their need.

Questions:

• What relationships in your life could benefit from greater truthfulness?

• What forms of deceit have been problematic for you and your relationships?

• How do you handle anger? How could seeing anger as potentially healthy impact the way you handle it in the future?

Chapter 11

Beware the Devil

"Be of sober spirit, be on the alert. Your adversary, the devil, prowls around like a roaring lion, seeking someone to devour. But resist him, firm in your faith, knowing that the same experiences of suffering are being accomplished by your brethren who are in the world."

1 Peter 5:8-9

While few would question the reality of evil in this world, the idea that there is a devil who can have direct influence on human lives is one not universally held, especially in first world countries. For many who hold to a western scientific worldview, talk of the demonic means delving into an archaic concept in a day and age when the social sciences have given us deeper insight into the human mind and emotions. But go to third world countries and it is a different story. Many there will describe evil spirits – demons if you will – and their impact on the lives of those who run afoul of them.

My own experience with the realm of the demonic has been a journey of discovery. I heard about the devil now and then as I grew up but never understood him to have any role other than that of a distant, evil concept that was somehow responsible for messing up human history. I have since come to realize that he is much more intimately involved in human affairs than I first realized. This chapter takes seriously the New Testament stories that describe the devil, his demons, and how they work to influence human lives. With this worldview in mind, any attempt to find freedom through forgiveness falls short unless demonic influence is recognized and dealt with. When it comes to the devil, ignorance is *not* a valid option.

The devil's fingerprints and demonic oppression

When it speaks of the devil, the Bible describes a malevolent, sentient, spiritual being named "Satan." His name means "adversary" and he is elsewhere also referred to as "the accuser" (Revelation 12:10). We see him first in Genesis 3, and from there periodically throughout scripture, always depicted as a specialist in the destruction of relationships. In Ephesians 4:25-27, Paul warns of a kind of demonic oppression that can dig so deep into a person's life that they need help to regain their freedom.

I first encountered this kind of oppression when I met Leona.

Leona's story

I received a phone call from a woman who wanted to talk to me. She said she had heard me speak at a recent event in the city. She asked if we could talk. I said that would be fine and we arranged to meet at a local coffee shop, a quiet but public venue.

From the moment we sat down, it was as though we were alone in the room, almost as if God had drawn a curtain around us. Surrounded by tables filled with other patrons, Leona told her story of abuse and betrayal. As she described what her abusive spouse had done to her over the years, her voice remained flat and her eyes dry. She had lived with her situation so long that there seemed to be no more emotion left and I commented on that. "I quit loving him years ago," she responded. "So why are you still with him?" I asked. It was evident that she did not want to be. "Money," she said. "I'm trapped with him because I don't have the money to leave."

I realized that I was wrong in thinking there was no emotion left. As she spoke, her bitterness began to surface and it became clear that Leona carried anger both at her husband for his betrayal and at God who seemed to do nothing to help her. She was bitter over her unanswered questions as to why this had happened to her and the years she had lost because of it. On top of it all, she saw no end in sight because her husband was not willing to change.

Like Leona, many of us have at some point felt trapped in a relationship. Our efforts to either change our situation or control the direction of our lives have failed and somewhere along the way we lost hope. Often God steps into this hopelessness in order to do something amazing. I was about to experience one of those amazing interventions as God stepped in to bring Leona back to freedom.

Unable to change her husband, Leona was stuck with him. What options did she have? I found myself prompted to ask a question: "Are you willing to forgive him?" She did not miss a beat. "No," she snapped.

I decided that I wanted to find out if Leona's "no" was absolute or if there might be some room to move. "Would you be willing to be made willing?" I asked. Leona stared at the table in front of her and I felt I could almost see her mind working, "Hmmm. If I'm willing to be made willing, then I don't have to *be* willing..."

Looking up, she said, "I'd be willing to be made willing."

"Okay," I responded, "let's pray that. Can I help you pray?" She looked at me. "Sure."

Often when I ask people to pray who, like Leona, have been struggling with long-term unforgiveness, I get a response to the effect that they have prayed but their prayers do not seem to work. I believe it is because those who have been in a place of struggle for a long time often default to the way of praying that they have become accustomed to. "Help me change him, Lord." "Make the pain go away, Lord." "Fix the situation, Lord." Quality of words is not where the problem lies, rather it is that God cannot make the pain go away unless change is made. Something *else* needs to be prayed. Repentance and belief need to be involved – a giving up of something, a letting go, or, as in Leona's case, a willingness to be made willing. This kind of prayer is an act of faith that allows God to bring the necessary change. I listened to Leona's story and, as I heard what she was holding onto and what she needed to let go of, I asked her if I could help that process. Having assured her that all she had to do was pour her heart into the prayer and hand it to God, I invited her to pray with me.

Leona bowed her head and the prayer we prayed went something like this: "Dear Jesus, I hate my husband and I feel trapped having to live with him. I don't know what to do. I'm being as honest as I can when I say he has hurt me so much that I'm not willing to forgive him. I've been angry at You too and I've blamed You for much of my pain, but I'm willing to be made willing to forgive. In Jesus' name. Amen."

Leona lifted her head and looked at me. For a moment, there was silence and I became aware that something miraculous was happening right in front of me as I saw the realization dawning in her eyes. She spoke, "This is just hurting *me*, isn't it?" It was more a statement than a question. "I might as well just forgive him and be done with it."

I was shocked at the speed with which we got our answer. "Leona, that was one of the fastest answers to prayer I've ever seen! Okay, let's pray that." Visibly excited over what had just happened, she bowed her head with me for the next prayer.

"Dear, Jesus. I invite You into the place of pain and anger I have over my husband."

The moment Leona got to the word "pain," she locked up. As I looked up at her, she looked helplessly back. Her lips moved. "There is a demon..." was all she could say. How she knew what it was, I could not say, but it prompted another question. "Do you want to get rid of it?" I asked. She nodded mutely. It was the permission Jesus needed to set her free. Taking her nod as a yes, I invited her, "Pray with me," and led her into prayer again. When we got to the point where she locked up, I spoke a command, "Evil spirit, I bind your power in Jesus' name and command you to let her speak."

It took significant effort, but Leona pushed the words of her prayer out through stiff lips, "Jesus, I invite You into my pain over my husband. I forgi…" She locked up again, and again I commanded the evil spirit to let her speak. "Pray with me, Leona." We persevered, understanding that the demon was trying to stop her from praying the prayer of repentance because it knew that once she had done so it would lose its grip on her life. My sense was that nothing was going to happen until that prayer of repentance had been prayed.

"Dear God, I forgive him, in Jesus' name, and I accept Your forgiveness for hating him. Forgive me for being angry at you, too." Leona slowly ground out the words through clenched teeth. With her repentance done, it was now Jesus' turn.

"Leona, you rest now," I said. The next part of the prayer was mine to do. In line with James' command to humble ourselves before God and resist the devil, Leona had humbled herself in her surrender to Jesus. It was now time to resist the devil and I named it for the issues in her life that it was wrapped around, "Spirit of unforgiveness and torment, she's forgiven her husband. Your power is broken and you have no more place in her life. In Jesus' name, I command you to go from Leona to where Jesus sends you." With those words, Leona's face twisted briefly and then relaxed. Tears flowed freely down her cheeks. She was free. When resisted in the context of humility before God and in the authority of Jesus' name, the devil had fled from her (James 4:7). We prayed then for the Spirit of Christ to fill the place in her life that the enemy had just let go of and we sat, enjoying the moment, while the people in the coffee shop around us continued on with what they were doing.

No one had even noticed what was going on right next to them.

This encounter was a clear and dramatic illustration of how the devil can sometimes find a place to oppress someone who chooses to actively nurture hatred rather than embracing the call to forgive. A number of factors were involved. Leona had suffered betrayal and abuse of her trust by her spouse. She had made the choice to actively nurture her hatred of her husband and, in the process of doing so, had given the devil opportunity to oppress her. But God intervened. He prepared her heart and enabled her to make her confession, empowering her as she renounced her bitterness and forgave her spouse. With her repentance complete, God stripped the demonic oppression from her life, filled her with the Holy Spirit, and gave her the freedom she was created for.

The devil works to divide

In order to do what he does, the devil needs something to work with. When we give him what he needs by making the selfish choice he tempts us with, he does his work effectively. He does his most effective work where relationships have broken down and he works without rest to further divide relationships so that he has more to work with. He works subtly if he can and openly if he has to. Even where there is no open demonic manifestation, we can often see signs of his handiwork, indicators that he has been messing around in a situation. Like any schemer does, he uses trickery, deceit, and manipulation in order to gain his ends. As far as the devil is concerned, when it comes to turning people against each other, anything goes. Forgiveness is God's strategy for dealing with the devil's influences and when we forgive from the heart the devil loses his power to take advantage of our situation:

"But one whom you forgive anything, I forgive also; for indeed what I have forgiven, if I have forgiven anything, I did it... so that no advantage would be taken of us by Satan, for we are not ignorant of his schemes."

2 Corinthians 2:10-11

By understanding that the devil's goal is to divide us through offenses, we can rob him of what he needs to do his work by making the choice to forgive.

Resist the devil

Understanding that there is a devil out there is one thing. Resisting the devil's attacks is another. The writer of the book of James acknowledges the existence of demonic power, the human selfishness that gives the devil his best place to work, and shows us the way to resist him.

"What causes fights and quarrels among you? Don't they come from your desires that battle within you? You desire but do not have, so you kill. You covet but you cannot get what you want, so you quarrel and fight. You do not have because you do not ask God. When you ask, you do not receive, because you ask with wrong motives, that you may spend what you get on your pleasures... "God opposes the proud but shows favor to the humble." Submit yourselves, then, to God. Resist the devil, and he will flee from you...Humble yourselves before the Lord, and he will lift you up."

James 4:1-3, 6-7, 10 NIV

As he teaches about pride, James says that God resists our efforts to live our lives by our own strength because, when we demand to do so, we keep God on the outside and doom ourselves to failure. This applies to the area of forgiveness as much as to any other aspect of our walk. We cannot fully forgive in our own strength because our pride keeps getting in the way. Whenever pride is the driving force behind our actions, what we might call forgiveness gets lost in our selfish attempts to manipulate the situation to our own ends. True forgiveness can only be accomplished where the motives behind it are selfless.

There is a scene in the movie "Schindler's List"[4] where the commandant of the concentration camp, Amon Goeth, is coached by Oscar Schindler to forgive the Jews he has in his camp, rather than punishing them every time one of them does something to offend his sense of authority. Schindler tells the commandant that the ability to forgive is a form of power greater than what the commandant wields when he uses lethal force. As the scene progresses, we see Goeth try to wrap his mind around this new "power." He tries an experiment in forgiveness with his Jewish houseboy who has just made a mistake while doing his work. Suppressing his rage, Goeth tells the houseboy that it is okay and that he "forgives" him. As the houseboy is dismissed and walks away from the house, something about Goeth's experiment in forgiveness does not satisfy his lust for power and control. He reverts to the way he knows best, picks up his rifle, steps out onto his balcony and shoots the boy, killing him for his mistake. Just as true forgiveness is not a form of personal power, neither can it be used to manipulate our situation. It can only be granted and received unconditionally as God gives us the strength.

The moment gaining power over our situation becomes the goal, we step into the realm of pride. Pride, in its basic essence, is self-dependence – "I'll do my life by my own strength for my own purposes and my own recognition." Pride puts us on the throne and in control of our destiny. Pride is what Adam and Eve were tempted with in the Garden when the devil essentially told them, "Bite this and you can be like God." As pride takes over, it eventually makes everything in our life and relationships all about us. Though our society glorifies pride, the writer of James says pride is the cause of our downfall, because it prevents us from depending on God and makes our prayers selfish and ineffective.

It also blocks us from being able to receive the help He wants to give us.

Humility is the opposite of pride. A humble person is not focused on punishing himself for his failings, nor is humility to be seen in self-degradation or self-abuse. Paul warns, "Speak evil of no man" (Titus 3:2 kjv). It took me some years to understand that we sin when we speak negatively about ourselves because we are degrading someone Christ died for. Don't do it! At its core, true humility is "God-dependence." A truly humble person lives life in God's strength, for His purposes and His glory, and finds it easy to accept God's help. However, a proud person cannot. Humility grows in us every time we forgive, because we are renouncing our ways for God's kingdom and will (See the Lord's Prayer in Matthew 6:9-13). When we live humbly, just as Jesus did, we live truly dependent on God and, from that foundational relationship, we can resist the devil and he must flee.

Away from me!

Jesus sometimes resisted the devil with a command.

Jesus said to him, "Away from me, Satan! For it is written: 'Worship the Lord your God, and serve him only.'"

Matthew 4:10 NIV

There are times when we are called to resist the devil, commanding him just as Jesus did with the authority Christ has granted to those who believe. It is important to acknowledge that the devil can sometimes influence lives filled with hatred. It is equally important to understand that the devil *does not have* power to control our lives forever. Nor does it mean we have to live in fear that one mistake or one immature tantrum will give him free access. Should he gain an opportunity in our lives, his access can simply and quickly be cancelled as we repent and trust once again in God's power and mercy. A person surrendered to Christ *can* resist the devil effectively. He no longer has to live in fear of being blindsided or oppressed by the demonic realm because he lives under the ongoing protection of God.

Degrees of influence

The point of Leona's story is not to say that everyone who carries a grudge is demonized, but to recognize that the devil can be a significant player in broken relationships, even to the point of direct demonic bondage. A careful study of the biblical accounts shows that there can be degrees of demonic influence. That means that the devil's involvement in broken relationships can sometimes be more invasive than at other times.

Like any effective predator, the devil stalks his prey, seeking an opening to do what he does best (1 Peter 5:8). Beginning his work from a distance, he takes the opportunities we give him and builds on them as we nurture our anger and hatred for those who have hurt us. How long ago Leona's oppression had started, I did not know, but over the years, as she actively cultivated her hatred of her husband, it had progressed into full-fledged demonic control. There *are* people who experience actual demonic oppression as a direct result of nurturing bitterness over betrayals done to them. That is why Paul cautions us with his bold command, "Neither give place to the devil" (Ephesians 4:27 kjv). Regardless of whether the devil simply exacerbates our situation from a distance, as he did with Vince in the previous chapter, or whether he has gained the kind of immediate grip that he had on Leona's life, a choice to take action and be done with nursing the anger has to be made. Even the willingness to be made willing to forgive allows God the opportunity He needs to do what He loves to do – bring freedom to those in need of it.

God has not given the devil the last say. Jesus cancelled his power through the forgiveness that He made possible at the cross. That forgiveness is at the core of living in freedom from the devil's influence. Christ gives that freedom to anyone who is willing to both receive it from Him and to take forgiveness on as a lifestyle (John 1:12). Again the question is: are we willing? Although God calls us to a place of choice, He will not override our personal determination to walk the road of our own choosing. If we want to walk in freedom, we must be willing to put what has been done to us in God's hands and forgive.

An important note:

Dealing with the demonic is a controversial topic, but an important one.

Poorly done teachings on the demonic have often left people demon-focused and living in fearful paranoia, convinced the devil is more powerful than he really is. The kind of biblically based teaching that factors things like demonic activity into the human struggle will often bring mockery from those who do not have a sound biblical worldview. Yet, I do not believe that ignorance is a valid option. I have chosen an approach that is centered on Christ more than on the devil, because keeping Jesus as our primary focus puts everything else into perspective, including the devil. Compared to Christ, the devil is absolutely powerless, because Christ defeated the devil's power at the cross (Colossians 2:14-15; Hebrews 2:14).

Christ is the source of the freedom we were made for, and increasing surrender to Him will bring increasing freedom from the works of the devil. If a person is willing to take his or her Bible seriously and, along with good mentorship and the Spirit's leading, apply the teachings of Jesus to real life situations and forgive, God will set them free.

I want to emphasize this again: when forgiveness is applied to a life gripped by demonic powers, Jesus cleanses and removes the sins that gave the demon its grip. When we forgive, we are giving Jesus the garbage in our lives that gives the demon its opportunity. No spiritual garbage means no chance of demonic oppression.

Finally, though we seek to understand, we need to resist the temptation to over-formulize things. Freedom is found in a relationship with Christ that is based on forgiveness and, though there is a process involved, it is much more than a formula of religion or a recipe for dealing with demons. Be careful of assuming something is demonic when you do not know. The best way to do this is to keep the focus on surrender to the Savior rather than on hunting for demons. Do not assume that someone is demonized just because they have a grudge. Focus rather on giving the grudge to Jesus, just as Leona did. As she surrendered what she carried to Jesus, God did the rest.

Questions:

• How have you viewed the devil and his potential to impact your life and relationships?

• What three insights did this chapter give you?

o ____
____

o ____
____

o ____
____

Chapter 12

What About When it Isn't Fair?

A friend of mine and I had a falling out. It was both one of the greatest and most difficult learning experiences of my life. Looking back on it, I think I could have handled it much differently, but at the time I did not know what I now know and did what came naturally.

There were misunderstandings. Accusations were made and actions taken. Suddenly I was no longer an asset but a threat to be dealt with. Thinking we could work it out, I called for meetings but they did not go well. I invited in a mediator and that did not go well either. Rather than making things better, everything got worse. Finally, as the last meeting drew to a close, I realized I had come up against a situation that I could not bring to a good resolution. More than just the failure of a professional relationship, it was the collapse of a deep, personal friendship and the pain was magnified accordingly. How could I continue to work alongside someone who had known me so well and yet now chose to follow such an unjust course of action over what, to me, were simple misunderstandings? At the time, the answer seemed pretty straightforward. Our relationship and work together were over.

I walked from there into a time of loneliness and pain. The joy disappeared from my life as I spent time obsessing over what had happened, what should have been done, and how unfair it all had been. My sense of injustice quickly turned to self-pity and began to cloud my perspective as the pain got worse. I had not done anything to deserve this. It was not fair! If only my friend would acknowledge the wrong that he had done and make things right, I was ready to forgive. But justice needed to be done first.

That was my condition – that justice be done. The wrong had to be acknowledged and made right. Looking back on it now, I have come to realize that my demand for justice was the main hurdle I had to get over in order to bring my situation to resolution. Getting to that point, though, would take time and pain as I walked a journey that would teach me much about what forgiveness really was. Insight came one morning several weeks into this experience as I fought the ever-present thoughts of how unfairly I had been handled. At the time, I happened to be reading the nineteenth chapter of the gospel of John.

Jesus accomplished justice so He could grant mercy

The Roman governor, Pontius Pilate, was agitated. He knew that something was wrong with the accusations being made against Jesus and that it was a setup but, try as he might, he could not get Jesus to speak in His own defense (Matthew 27:18). On top of that, the more Pilate tried to find a non-lethal solution to the accusations against Jesus, the more demanding and confrontational the accusers of Jesus became.

"Pilate said to [Jesus' accusers], "You take him and crucify him. As for me, I find no basis for a charge against him." The Jewish leaders insisted, "We have a law, and according to that law he must die, because he claimed to be the Son of God." When Pilate heard this, he was even more afraid, and he went back inside the palace. "Where do you come from?" he asked Jesus, but Jesus gave him no answer. "Do you refuse to speak to me?" Pilate said. "Don't you realize I have power either to free you or to crucify you?" Jesus answered, "You would have no power over me if it were not given to you from above. Therefore the one who handed me over to you is guilty of a greater sin."

John 19:6-11 NIV

Contrary to what some may say about Pilate, being a Roman governor did not give him complete freedom to simply execute people without cause. Governors who butchered too many people had riots, and riots not only cost Rome money for more troops but also made it look like the governor did not have what it took to keep order. It did not go well for governors who allowed too many riots. Charged with ruling a people well known for uprisings, Pilate understood how another riot could negatively affect his career. He wanted nothing more than to let Jesus go and for the crisis to pass. To that end, he tried to get Jesus to defend Himself.

But Jesus refused.

In that moment, I saw the passage with new eyes. There was something bigger than simple justice going on here. It struck me that had Jesus simply opened His mouth and spoken the truth – that He was innocent of the charges against Him – Pilate, who was already certain that Jesus was being falsely accused, would have let Him go. Had Jesus been released, there would have been no cross and no crucifixion, no death and no resurrection. Sin would have been left undefeated and salvation would not have been accomplished. The devil would have been left with his power intact and all humanity would be eternally lost.

So Jesus kept silent. With His focus set on going to the cross, He had a greater purpose in mind than simply getting fair treatment for Himself. There He would accomplish God's justice by dying an unjust death in order to pay for our guilt with His innocence. Having done so, He would rise from the dead with power to grant mercy simply as a gift to be received by all who were willing (Titus 3:4-7; Ephesians 2:4-8). I realized then that Jesus had kept His mouth shut in front of Pilate so that I might be given the mercy I needed rather than the condemnation I deserved.

I have come to learn that forgiveness is not about getting fair treatment. It is about mercy.

It was a significant insight and the first of several major realizations I needed to come to as God prepared me for the next stage of my growth.

To sue or not to sue?

As I struggled to decide what I should do next, I went to two professional counselors looking for some help. After hearing my situation, both counselors told me to get a lawyer and pursue legal action. They were logical and made a good case, saying that the way in which I was being handled was unprofessional and abusive. Not only had it cost me personally in terms of emotional pain, but it had also hurt my career once word had gotten out into the community about the accusations made against me by my old friend and associate.

Legal action made sense and seemed justified, but I could not get any peace over making the choice to pursue that option. As I prayed and deliberated over it, asking God to show me what to do, an obscure New Testament passage came to mind:

"Does any one of you, when he has a case against his neighbor, dare to go to law before the unrighteous and not before the saints? Or do you not know that the saints will judge the world? If the world is judged by you, are you not competent to constitute the smallest law courts? Do you not know that we will judge angels? How much more matters of this life? So if you have law courts dealing with matters of this life, do you appoint them as judges who are of no account in the Church? I say this to your shame. Is it so, that there is not among you one wise man who will be able to decide between his brethren, but brother goes to law with brother, and that before unbelievers? Actually, then, it is already a defeat for you, that you have lawsuits with one another. Why not rather be wronged? Why not rather be defrauded?"

1 Corinthians 6:1-7

Paul's words challenged the very logical advice that I had received and changed my perspective. As a follower of Christ, I had claimed to believe in Jesus' call to forgive and love my enemies. Was I now supposed to take my friend to court? Doing so seemed justifiable, but at the same time it seemed wrong. The words from 1 Corinthians came back to me over and over: "It is already a defeat for you, that you have lawsuits with one another. Why not rather be wronged? Why not rather be defrauded?"

I could not get any peace over pursuing legal options.

Keeping my mouth shut, and the question "why?"

As I processed what I was going through, I took long prayer walks – though I probably prayed less and obsessed more about what had been done, could have been done, or should have been done. As I walked, I found myself struggling to reconcile my need for justice with my desire to find peace. During this time, another New Testament passage began to come to mind over and over again:

"For this finds favor, if for the sake of conscience toward God a person bears up under sorrows when suffering unjustly. For what credit is there if, when you sin and are harshly treated, you endure it with patience? But if when you do what is right and suffer for it you patiently endure it, this finds favor with God. For you have been called for this purpose, since Christ also suffered for you, leaving you an example for you to follow in His steps, who committed no sin, nor was any deceit found in His mouth; and while being reviled, He did not revile in return; while suffering, He uttered no threats, but kept entrusting Himself to Him who judges righteously..."

1 Peter 2:19-23

As the Apostle Peter's words continued to come to mind, they began to unfold in more depth and with greater application to my situation. Christ was accused unjustly and kept his mouth shut while going through what He went through. He did so as an act of faith, trusting that God had some good purpose in allowing what was happening to Him. Anyone can suffer for breaking the law but Jesus suffered without cause. The passage said that God values it when, as an act of faith, we trust Him with our situation while making the choice to suffer unjustly rather than giving in to the temptation to defend ourselves. Peter went on to say that we who follow Jesus are also called, at times in our lives, to walk in the way that Jesus walked and to adopt the kind of action that He adopted because it allows us a taste of what Jesus went through.

Please do not hear me wrong. I am not saying we should keep our mouth shut every time something bad happens to us, nor am I saying that we should encourage abuse by our silence. If a child is being abused by a predator, or a woman by an abusive husband, we need to speak up in the interest of protecting those victims. That said, there are times in our personal growth where we will be called to deal with injustice by keeping our mouths shut and trusting God with the situation. Peter says in the above passage, "For you have been called for this purpose..."

I was called for this purpose? What does keeping my mouth shut have to do with my growth? The book of James says it well:

"Consider it all joy, my brethren, when you encounter various trials, knowing that the testing of your faith produces endurance. And let endurance have its perfect result, so that you may be perfect and complete, lacking in nothing."

James 1:2-4

I read this passage over and over again. What was God's reason in asking me to embrace the pain, trust Him with the situation, and keep my mouth shut? What if God did not make things happen the way I wanted them to happen? Was I willing to trust that God knew what He was doing and that He could bring some good out of it anyway? Whatever He was doing, He certainly was not fixing the pain. I had always thought that obedience to God would bring peace, but it did not in this situation. It was hard to be silent, not knowing how to resolve an issue that I did not understand. This was not the way I had envisioned it would be when I set out to follow God's call on my life.

Keeping on trusting

Our natural response when suffering is to focus on the source of the pain and do what we have to do to make it stop. Jesus chose a different way, having made it clear to His disciples that He did not have to go through with the cross and that He did what He was doing voluntarily. He could have opted out but chose not to, choosing instead to persevere, regardless of the pain. The Bible goes on to say that Jesus endured the cross for the sake of what was to be accomplished through it, trusting God for the blessing that lay beyond the pain (Matthew 26:53-54; Hebrews 12:2).

While being cursed and unjustly treated, Jesus refused to defend Himself but held his silence and "kept entrusting Himself" into the hands of God (1 Peter 2:23). Many Bible translations make it sound as though His choice to trust was a single act – He "trusted," as though His act of trusting only lasted for a moment. The New American Standard Bible translates the original Greek verb as an act that had a starting point and then carried on. It says that He "*kept entrusting* Himself." This was an important distinction to me because it taught me that trusting God is more than a momentary thing. Trust is something that can require perseverance. This was certainly Jesus' experience. The journey from His arrest to the cross took time and, though He was frequently tempted to quit, He refused to opt out, persevering in trusting God right to the end.

I realized that God had me in a process of learning to trust Him but that my tendency toward taking the easy way made me want to bail out before the journey was complete. Once I came to realize that bailing out too early would thwart what He wanted to accomplish, it got to the point that all I knew was that God was good and He was somehow in control. I, too, was being called to *keep on* entrusting myself and my situation into the hands of God.

When is the pain over?

"When is the pain going to be over, Lord?" was the question I asked

God one day as I was out for my prayer walk. His response came quickly in the form of a strong, clear thought: "It will be over when it is over."

It will be over when it is over?! What did *that* mean? That was not the answer I was looking for.

Thank God that He takes our immaturity into account. He did so with me that day. God works with us where we are at because it is sometimes all He has to work with as He draws us into deeper maturity. Again the thought came: "I have a purpose. Trust me. It will be over when it is over. You cannot read your way into maturity, you know."

That hit home! Good point, because I had a bookshelf of self-help books and had been trying to do exactly that, thinking that if I could learn from the mistakes of other people I might be able to circumnavigate some of the challenges I would otherwise have to face the hard way. But maturity cannot happen without allowing enough time for the pain of our situation to develop our ability to hold our priorities and keep our focus in the midst of the adversity. Like an athlete's body develops through the discipline of hard training, we grow in spiritual and emotional maturity as we learn to deal with the stress and responsibility of life and leadership without losing our trust in God. As I looked at maturity in light of the biblical injunction to consider it a joy when trials and testings come (James 1:1-2), I was reminded of the process used to refine gold.

The refining process

Like people, gold is never found in its purest form. It is always mixed with other impurities. These are removed by a process known as refining.

In preparing gold for the jeweler's use, the refiner places the impure gold into a high-heat container. The fire is turned up under the container until the gold melts. Knowing that the impurities in the gold do not separate out either quickly or easily – due to the thick viscosity of the molten metal – the refiner keeps the heat high long enough for the gold to settle to the bottom and the impurities to rise to the surface. By the time the separation is complete, and depending on the amount of the impurities present, the gold can become totally obscured by the dross that now floats on its surface. When the refiner judges the separation to be complete, he shuts the heat off. As the metal cools and the gold hardens, so does its surface layer of impurities. The final step is to shave the layer of dross off the cooled block of metal, revealing a brick of clean, pure gold ready for the jeweler's use.

The image made sense to me. There were parallels between my situation and the refining process. I saw my tendency to trust myself rather than God. I also saw my tendencies toward anger, self-pity, and blaming others for what was happening to me. All of my ugly immaturities came to the surface as God allowed my pain to become the fire that refined me.

Just as my heart had to be changed if I was to be made ready for the next part of my walk as a servant of Christ, so the motives of each of our hearts must change if we are to mature and become equipped to help others. Self-ishness has to be replaced by self-lessness. If Jesus Himself was made perfect through suffering (Hebrews 2:10), then who was I to expect that I could be used by God without going through some of what Jesus went through? I could change careers and friends easily enough but I could not change my own heart. Only God could do that and, even for God, there was no way around the refiner's fire. For now all I could do was endure, and so the journey continued as God prepared me for the next step in the "repent and believe" process. For me, that meant laying down the weapons I had used as I struggled to get my own way.

Recognizing the instruments of revenge

We all have our weapons – ways that we use either to pay back those who have hurt us or to punish them until they come over to our way of thinking. I discovered that I had mine and was well versed in their use. I also found out that I was so used to using them, I did not even recognize when I was doing so.

"You're rejecting him just like you feel he has rejected you." The statement my wife had made earlier in the evening stuck with me as I got my jacket and stepped out the door to take my son to his soccer practice. Her words were not what I wanted to hear. Didn't she understand what I was going through? Where was the support and compassion?

It was after dark by the time we arrived at the soccer field and the playing surface was illuminated by overhead lights. Standing back from the sidelines, just out of the glare, I found my thoughts wandering back to what my wife had said. "You're rejecting him just like you feel he has rejected you." As the truth of her words sank in, I had a mental image of myself standing with an automatic rifle in my hands – a military weapon designed specifically for killing. As the scene played in my mind, I saw myself bend over and lay the weapon on the ground. As I straightened up and looked down, I saw the weapon suddenly coated with what I knew to be the blood of Jesus, all of its highlights clearly visible. Suddenly the blood soaked into the ground, taking the weapon with it. Very quickly it was gone from my sight, leaving behind only a bare patch of grass along with a thought that I believe was the voice of God: "I have taken your weapons away."

Immediately I knew that what my wife had said was true. I had become so accustomed to rejecting others who I felt were rejecting me that punishing people by rejecting them back had become a reflex action. As I saw my tendency to default to my old cycle, often without even really recognizing that I was doing so, I knew God was calling me to handle this relationship differently. I had to renounce treating my friend as I felt he had treated me. I watched my worldly weapon sink into the ground, wondering what was to come next.

Worldly weapons take many forms. There are physical weapons, like guns and knives and clubs. There are also emotional weapons that may be familiar to us, such as gossip, intimidation, deceit, character assassination, blame-shifting, playing the victim role in order to get pity from others – or the silent treatment where we ignore someone in order to punish them. Paul says that followers of Jesus do not use such weapons but that our weapons are spiritual. Faith in Christ, the Word of God, the authority of the name of Jesus, the blood of Christ shed on the cross, prayer, and forgiveness, these are the weapons we bring to the fight.

"For though we walk in the flesh, we do not war according to the flesh, for the weapons of our warfare are not of the flesh, but divinely powerful for the destruction of fortresses."

2 Corinthians 10:3-4

When it comes to weapons, using sin to deal with sin gets us nowhere. The old saying, "Two wrongs don't make a right," is very true. As long as our focus is on paying back the one who has hurt us, we cannot see the true picture of what is going on, nor can we obtain a good outcome to our situation. We need to renounce the old weapons that we are used to and take up the weapons of Christ.

God's purpose is the restoration of relationships through forgiveness (Matthew 22:37-40). Having poured His mercy out on us through what Jesus did on the cross, God also desires to pour that mercy through us to each other. As He changes our perspective about our weapons and their use, God calls us to a new understanding of our enemies and of the one who is really behind them. Part of forgiving often includes an acknowledgement that those who have hurt us are not our primary enemy and that the true enemy is the devil who is trying to capitalize on our situation by turning us against each other (Ephesians 6:11-12).

The tipping point

My prayer walks continued and the pain went on. Though I was gaining new insight into what it meant to forgive, I was unable to sit at home, so I pounded the pavement daily. I put many miles on my running shoes as I walked, prayed, and continued to struggle with the desire to understand.

I still wanted to know why this had all happened and I felt that if only I knew the "why," then I could endure.

The moment of breakthrough came one morning as I was out walking. It felt as though something suddenly shifted inside and I had finally had enough, "Lord, I don't care why it happened anymore. I just need Your mercy." As I prayed those words, something changed. It was as if someone had punched a hole in my bucket of pain and it all began to drain away. The "why" was no longer important and the only thing that mattered now was that I and my situation were in God's hands. Though nothing changed outwardly and no one came to apologize or to say that a mistake had been made, a certain peace began to settle in and I gained a new ability to live without pain.

It was the pain and my inability to help myself that finally changed the way I prayed. Prior to the tipping point, all my prayers had been selfish and demanding, driven by the pain of my situation. I had put conditions on God, demanding that He explain to me why this had happened to me, and my conditions had made me unable to move forward. After the tipping point, it was different. Now I prayed "Mercy, Lord." I did not care about the "why" anymore; I just needed to be at God's mercy. I had reached the point of surrender and was ready to let go of demanding my own agenda. As my heart made the shift from demanding that God explain Himself and just surrendered to His mercy, I gained the freedom to step forward out of the pain.

Shortly after the tipping point occurred, my wife and I were out at a movie and, while I do not remember the movie we saw, I do remember that at some point during the show my thoughts were distracted from the screen in front of me by a progression of images that went through my mind. I saw a stream with a small bridge over it, along with the accompanying thought, "like water under the bridge."

I was instantly aware that the picture referred to my situation and I knew right away what it meant. God was saying to me that my situation was like water under the bridge. It was gone. It was over. My efforts to bring my situation back to where it could be "properly dealt with" were like trying to bucket water that had already flowed downstream, back up to the bridge. It was futile. It could not be done. With every bucket of water I hauled back upstream, the rest disappeared farther and farther downriver. Even as I dumped one bucket on the upstream side of the bridge and raced downstream for more, the water I had just hauled upstream passed me again on its way back downstream. In that moment, I knew that all hope of "fixing" the offense between me and my friend was gone. The peace was palpable. I did not have to fix anything. I could finally quit striving and just let it all go.

As I reflected on the images I was seeing, another thought came to my mind, "What if I just tell him I forgive him and ask his forgiveness for any way in which I might have hurt him? What if I tell him I have no strings attached and then just re-engage where the relationship left off?" The thought seemed ridiculous. I had seen his anger, was sure he hated me, and was convinced that he would not be interested in re-engaging any kind of a relationship. Just to be safe, I thought I had better check it out by bouncing it off my wife. I shared my experience with her after the show, expecting her to agree that it had just been my imagination. Instead, she looked at me for a long moment then said, "I think God is speaking to you."

Great! Now what? Had God actually spoken to me and then used my wife to confirm it? This whole experience had been really painful and I finally felt ready to move on from it. In no way was I going to open myself up for more pain without being sure of what I thought I was hearing. The only option I could think of was to phone my friend and ask him out for coffee. "No problem," I thought. "He hates me and he'll say no." I was sure he would refuse my request out of hand.

I punched his personal number into my phone, hoping for his voicemail so I could leave a message. Instead I heard his voice as he answered the phone. I identified myself and asked if he would like to go out for a coffee. To my amazement, he said, "Yes." In a bit of a fog, I suggested a time and place. Great! Now I had to come up with something to say.

We met at the appointed time, bought our coffee, and chose a seat by the windows away from the other customers in the café. Nervously, my friend made some small talk for a few minutes and then there was a moment of quiet. It was the opportunity I had been waiting for and I spoke into the silence. Not sure of how to preface what I needed to say, I quietly asked God for wisdom and chose the direct approach: "I asked you to come here so that I can say I forgive you for everything you've said or done to me." He looked at me without speaking and I continued, "I also want to ask your forgiveness for anything I said or did to hurt you." I was not totally innocent either in the sense that I had also said some harsh things at one of our previous meetings. I went on to say that I had no expectations of a response from him if he did not want to give one, and I told him that I was still his friend.

The silence settled between us as I finished what I had to say. After several seconds it became a little uncomfortable and, in an effort to lighten the moment, I added, "We can cry now if we want to." To my amazement, he reached out and took my hand as tears filled his eyes and began to slide down his cheeks. As I watched Him sit quietly, his jaw working as he sought to contain his emotion, I realized I had been so consumed by my own struggle over what had happened that, in my self-centeredness, all I had been able to see was my own pain. I had not thought of how my friend might also be hurting over what had transpired between us. As I looked into his eyes, I knew that it had hurt him as much as it had hurt me. This man was my friend and my brother, and we had wounded one another.

We parted company and I did not really know what was going to happen next, but I found myself praising God for how He had intervened. I understood more deeply why He is called the Redeemer – the One who takes what is meant for evil and brings good from it (Genesis 50:20). God had allowed my situation and refused to let me simply "fix it" so I could move on. There was too much I needed to learn.

God demonstrated that He can bring back hope when everything seems hopeless. He used everything that had happened to good effect. None of the pain was wasted and, in the midst of my struggle, when all I could see was my need for fair treatment, God taught me that forgiveness is not about fair treatment but about mercy, and that forgiving can only be done when the heart is ready. I learned that redeeming the pain and growing deeper in my relationships can sometimes require enduring a wrong with patience. As He revealed to me His heart for my friend and I, God demonstrated His faithfulness and taught me to surrender to Him in the midst of one of the most difficult and painful situations that I had ever experienced. It taught me that those we love are worth more than the offenses that we so often allow to come between us.

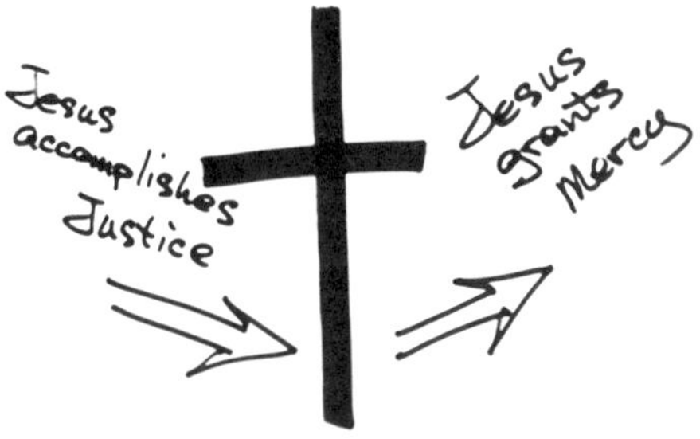

The journey I had just come through with my friend gave me a profoundly deepened understanding of the cross of Jesus and what had happened there. Jesus did what we could not do. In the place where injustice and eternal death ruled, Jesus accomplished justice for us, replacing the rule of sin and death with the rule of God's love, mercy, and eternal life (Romans 8:2). In His suffering on the cross, He demonstrated God's desire to pour out His mercy on us, much as a parent lavishes her love on an infant who can do nothing but receive the love poured out. He wanted me to have the experience of being able to offer the mercy I had received to someone else who also needed it. The only way I could do that was from a place of injustice. There were some uncomfortable dinners ahead with my friend and his family, as we figured out how to re-engage our relationships with each other, but the hard part was over.

I came out of this experience with several new insights:

I learned that people naturally demand fair treatment and that this demand is often the biggest obstacle to moving ahead into freedom. God is not fair, at least not in the way we often understand "fair." God is merciful, and living by the mercy of God is a part of the call of a follower of Jesus.

I learned that when we demand fair treatment, we demand something that is not always in the heart of God to give. If God treated us fairly, we would get the eternal punishment we deserve. Thank God He treats us mercifully rather than fairly. In coming to see the crucifixion of Jesus as something He did because it was necessary to make possible the forgiveness I needed, I began to see the cross as an expression of His extreme mercy.

Even as I learned that God is not fair, I learned that the devil is not fair either. As the apex spiritual predator, Satan uses every opportunity he can get in order to turn God's beloved children against one another. We cannot play his game and win.

I saw just how natural it is for us to act out of our own selfishness while thinking we are in the right. Every time I opened my mouth, I demonstrated what was most important to me – my wounded pride, my pain, my image. How could I give anything to others when everything was all about what I needed to get first? I came to realize how important it was for my growth to learn how to keep my mouth shut.

Looking back on the experience, I did not do a real good job of emulating what Jesus did when He kept quiet before Pontius Pilate, because every time I opened my mouth it was in my own defense or to demand justice. I soaked myself in self-pity and the pain of the betrayal I felt I had suffered, while over and over I hammered at God with my demands for an explanation. The predominant questions on my mind when I prayed were, "Why?" "What did I do to deserve this?" "Why did You allow it to happen?" It was always all about me.

I learned that the pain has a purpose. After a time, the pain changes what we value. Prior to the tipping point – when my prayers changed from demanding an explanation to simply asking for mercy – justice for myself and vindication of my reputation were most important to me. The pain changed all that and gave me a new perspective, causing me to re-evaluate what was of real consequence. I came to the conclusion that much of what I used to value simply did not matter anymore. The only thing of any real importance was to be in the hands of God and receiving His mercy.

I learned the value of silence. Keeping silent lifts our focus from our situation to our Savior. When we no longer depend on our ability to explain, understand, or fix things, we begin to depend on His ability to lead us through what lies ahead. It changes our character by making us less self-centered and gives us experience in depending on Him regardless of circumstances. Having seen our own weaknesses, we gain an ability to empathize that we never had before. That also makes us less judgmental because we are no longer able to condemn those who have failed as we have. Someone who does not condemn becomes a safe place for a struggling person to come to.

Growing in maturity

I also gained a deeper understanding of maturity. As my friend and I struggled with one another, we demonstrated our true levels of maturity by the way we reacted to each other. I found that I had a picture of what

I expected my friend to act like, just as he had one of me. In our struggle, we proved that neither he nor I were as mature as we had thought ourselves to be. Because we could not demand each other to be more mature than we were, the only other option we had was to change our expectations and learn how to give each other room to grow.

The journey that Jesus led His disciples on was one of learning ongoing trust. Knowing that trust did not come naturally to them, He led them situation by situation into places where they were in over their heads and then asked them to depend on Him there. Over and over He proved His faithfulness to them by never letting them down. They learned to trust Him just as He Himself trusted His Heavenly Father. All we do, including giving and receiving forgiveness, must be grounded in trusting God and in looking to Him for the outcome.

Do not get me wrong. The call to trust God is not a call to passivity. Neither is the call to forgive those who have hurt us. Jesus was a man of action above all else, someone who did what had to be done and His action took Him to the cross. Confronted every step of the way with the temptation to abandon His calling, He made the choice to keep on trusting. He looked through His situation rather than being distracted by it, and the knowledge that His actions would make freedom available to all drew Him on.

"Therefore, since we are surrounded by such a great cloud of witnesses, let us throw off everything that hinders and the sin that so easily entangles. And let us run with perseverance the race marked out for us, fixing our eyes on Jesus, the pioneer and perfecter of faith. For the joy set before him he endured the cross, scorning its shame, and sat down at the right hand of the throne of God."

Hebrews 12:1-2 NIV

Questions:

• What have you learned from the pain you have experienced in your relationships?

• How have you handled the temptation to demand fair treatment?

• Which insight from this chapter speaks most directly to a relationship you are struggling with? How? What course of action might you need to take?

Chapter 13

The End of "Self"

Understanding mercy begins when we come to the end of "self." At the end of self, those who are willing to say "yes" to Christ experience that God is more faithful to us than we can ever be to Him, and that He has led us into a difficult place in order to ready us for what only He can give. There God breaks down the selfish agendas that have prevented us from being able to receive the mercy we need. I came to understand this the day that I cursed God.

On the slopes of Kilimanjaro

It was banana country. The hillsides around us were covered with lush foliage spreading up the slopes into the mist that still hung over the higher elevations. Above that, the snow-covered peak of Tanzania's Mount Kilimanjaro soared majestically into the skies of East Africa. After two weeks of bush preaching in the Katavi region, a team of pastors, including myself, traveled by truck back to Mwiki, located on the lower slopes of Kilimanjaro. There I would spend my last week in-country teaching a pastors' seminar. One of the sessions I had prepared was the story of Peter's denial and how Jesus afterward confronted him on the beach with the question, "Peter, do you love Me?"

My goal was to get at the heart of how Jesus showed Peter that he could not live out his calling on his own strength. I planned to emphasize how much we are like Peter. Because of our tendency to try to live life in our own strength, often God has to take us to a place of being beyond our abilities so we can finally experience the magnitude of our weakness and the extreme nature of God's love for us. It is the place where performance fails and faith begins as we discover the forgiveness that does not end and the God who cannot let us down.

There were about 200 pastors in the room that morning. The sun shone through the windows and the greenery of the banana plantation bordering our compound was visible as I settled my books on the podium. My translator stepped to my side and, after opening with a short prayer, I began to speak of the story of Peter's betrayal and restoration from John 21.

Peter had made his commitment to Jesus and, yet, when it came time to take his stand, he failed His best friend and Lord. He also failed himself. His inability to live up to his commitment to Christ bred in him a sense of despair and guilt that stayed with him through the crucifixion and beyond the resurrection. Convinced that he did not have what it took to follow Jesus anymore, his shame drove him to abandon his calling and return to the only life he really knew – fishing. It was here that Jesus came looking for him and here that Christ asked His famous question, "Peter, do you love Me?"

In the original Greek text of the Bible, two words for "love" are used in this passage. The first is the word philia and the second agapé. Philia describes the give-and-take love that grows between brothers. Though an intense form of love, it does not have the same depth and unconditionality as agapé. Agapé is the word used to describe the heart of God as expressed in Christ. It is the kind of love that Jesus demonstrated on the cross as He prayed, "Father, forgive them; for they know not what they are doing" (Luke 23:34). Demanding nothing in return, it just loves regardless of the response it gets.

Some scholars think John used these two Greek words for love interchangeably but I am not so sure. If we allow that John, when he wrote his gospel, used these two different words deliberately, the conversation between Jesus and Peter takes on a greater depth of meaning. In effect, the interchange between Jesus and Peter would have gone something like this:

“When they had finished eating, Jesus said to Simon Peter, “Simon son of John, do you love Me unconditionally?

Do you really love Me more than these others do?”

Peter replied, “Lord, You know I love You as though You were my brother.” Jesus said, “Feed My lambs.” Jesus then deliberately asked the question again, using repetition as a way of focusing attention and making a point: “Peter, do you love Me unconditionally, just as I have loved you?”

Peter responded, “Lord, You know I love You as though You were my own brother.” Jesus said, “Feed my sheep.”

For a third time Jesus asked his question, but now he changed the word he used from agapé to philia. He asked, “Peter, do you love Me like a brother?” Peter was hurt when, the third time, Jesus asked him if he loved Him like a brother because the question emphasized that he did not love Jesus unconditionally. Why was Jesus pressing this point? In essence, when Peter responded to Jesus’ third question by saying again that he loved Jesus like a brother, he was admitting openly that he did not have what it took to love Jesus like Jesus loved him.

“What do You want me to say, Lord? I know I failed You. I know You love me more than I love You. You know everything, Lord. I do love You but it was not enough to prevent me from betraying You.”

Prior to his betrayal, Peter had actually claimed to love Jesus more deeply than all the rest of the disciples put together. He had declared that he was ready to go anywhere and endure anything for the sake of his commitment to his Lord. Even if everyone else ran, he would be faithful. Yet, when the time came, he failed. His weakness and fear turned out to be stronger than he had expected, while his commitment was shown to be not as strong as he had thought.

Peter stood on the beach before Jesus with the wound of his betrayal laid bare and his self-loathing at the surface for all to see. Into his weakness, Jesus spoke, "Take care of my sheep." He went on to tell Peter that a time was coming when he would be led to serve God in a way that he never would have chosen for himself and that God would be glorified in him. Jesus knew that Peter could never follow Him on the strength of his own commitment, but Peter needed to know that, too. In allowing Peter to be led into a situation where his own strength was not enough, Jesus showed him his inability and taught him that the strength to serve God would come from God himself. Peter had to learn that all he could do was offer God what he had and trust the Spirit of God to carry him. Jesus let Peter know that what he had to give was enough and, with his greatest failure met by God's mercy, Peter finally understood that there was more to following Jesus than emotional declarations and personal determination.

In the way He handled Peter, Jesus demonstrated to those who followed Him that a relationship with God was more about God's faithfulness than about the ability of His disciples to be strong in their service. Jesus does not choose the strong or the supremely gifted to be His followers. He chooses the weak and empowers those whom He chooses (1 Corinthians 1:27). Once chosen, He never gives up on them.

The morning session drew to a close. Soon we would have lunch and shortly after that would be the afternoon break-out sessions. Looking out over the gathered pastors, I closed my presentation with these comments: "I've gained some understanding of what happened on that beach between Peter and Jesus. I, too, cursed God and yet He still uses me." We were dismissed for lunch.

That afternoon our team leader shared with me that the pastors had asked me if I could come up with another Bible study for the next morning. I replied that I thought I could.

The next day dawned bright and cool, with the mist retreating back up the mountainside as the sun began to burn off the fog that was so common to mornings in that place. Breakfast was a bowl of chicken broth with a full chicken leg lying in it. Eggs, ugali (a glutinous mass of cooked maize porridge), papayas fresh from the tree, and strong, black, instant coffee rounded out the fare. It was wonderful. After breakfast was finished, we gathered to begin our sessions.

I took my place behind the small podium and the translator echoed my words in Swahili as I prayed, asking the Spirit of God to anoint us for the teaching at hand. With the "Amen," I opened my mouth to begin.

Before I could speak, an elderly pastor seated two rows from the front and off to my left stood and addressed me: "Pastor, you said yesterday that you cursed God and yet you still serve Him. We want you to tell us about this."

I was brought up short. What should I say? I had not planned to share anything about that. Moreover, what would they think of me if I were to tell that story? In my mind, these were not run-of-the-mill, everyday people I was speaking to. These were African pastors, and I felt they were a very special breed. They ministered in Churches that were experiencing explosive growth and knew both sides of what it meant to follow Christ. On one hand, they knew revival, while on the other had seen trials of a magnitude that I had never faced myself. I felt that they had a much greater depth of holiness than I did and I was not sure if my story would translate into their language and culture without totally invalidating my standing as a man of God in their eyes.

The question hung in the silence. In that moment I wished that I had never mentioned it. The pastor who had given the request stood looking at me, awaiting my response. I answered that I would do my best. He sat down and the room became very quiet. I sent up a quick prayer for mercy and began by sharing that the story of my cursing God was a story of God's faithfulness in the midst of my own unfaithfulness.

Cursing God

I began my pastoral career, young and idealistic. Things went well and the ministry I was involved with saw many become new believers while many others committed to a deeper walk with Christ. I was determined to follow the Lord come what may, but, like Peter, I was naïve and things happened that I had not anticipated. As my unrealistic picture of what the ministry was like began to fail me, my frustration, stress, and disillusionment began to pile up.

Rather than learning how to be honest with God about where I was at, I had been taught that people who really serve Jesus are not allowed to get angry. As many before me have come to realize, I discovered the hard way that, for those who try to stuff their anger, there comes a day when there is no more room to put it and no more energy to try. Ten years into the ministry, disappointment and disillusionment with the Christian Church had brought me to the end of my ability to serve Christ. I had just gone through a burnout experience and I was feeling very alone. The challenges facing me seemed insurmountable and I did not know what to do or where to go next. I was depressed, filled with despair and anger.

One evening, I told my wife I was going out for a walk. It was dark and a light rain was falling as I walked down the middle of an empty side street. Poorly illuminated houses were set well back from the sidewalks on either side of the road and I was alone in the cold dampness of the night. With my spiritual life both exhausted and exhausting, the romance of following Jesus was gone. All I could see were the failures. As I walked, I began to pour out my heart to God. Gradually my prayers began to increase in volume, finally rising to shouts as my anger and disillusionment began to boil over. Anyone nearby would have easily heard my railing. With the floodgates of my bottled-up anger having finally burst, I cursed my life and service to God using every expletive I knew.

Looking back on it, I now realize that, in my anger and cursing, I was actually being more real with God than I had been in a long time. Rather than just trying to gather my strength and push forward, I was finally ready to openly show Him what was in my heart. It was not pretty, but at least it was honest. I bluntly said I was done serving Him, that He should leave me alone and go find someone else to use. Once my venting had run its course, I settled into an angry silence. In that moment came a clear, definitive thought and I knew it was God speaking to me: "This is sin, you know."

"I know that!" I shot back.

The thought came again, "Do you think that you should ask for forgiveness?"

"Go ahead if You want to!" My response came out of my anger and mirrored my inability to perform any longer. I think what I was saying was something like, "You can do whatever You want to, Lord. I don't have what it takes to try anymore."

The thought came one more time, "Okay. I will." End of conversation.

Emotionally spent, I quietly walked the two blocks home. It was late as I pulled off my clothes and crawled into bed alongside my wife. As far as I was concerned, my service to God was at an end. When tomorrow came I would begin the process of seeking another career and another way of living.

I awoke to the sound of ringing, stumbled out of bed, and groggily answered the old-style rotary phone mounted on the wall in my office. The person on the other end of the line introduced herself and stated the reason for her call. Would I be willing to come and do a three-day youth speaking engagement at a boarding school out East? I found myself saying, "Yes," took the dates, said goodbye, and hung up the receiver. Still waking up, I suddenly remembered the previous evening as I tried to process what had just happened. "Lord, I thought I was finished. What's going on?" Again the thought came clearly, as it had the night before, and again I knew it to be the voice of God: "You might be done with Me, but I'm not done with you."

The journey is hard

It was silent in the room as I came to the end of my story. I looked out over the Tanzanian pastors gathered in the hall that morning and closed by saying, "That's when I learned that I can't follow God in my own strength. Trying to serve Him out of my own strength was my problem. Though I knew Christ, though I had said "yes" to a relationship with Him, though I had been filled with the Spirit and received gifts for use in ministry, I still did not know how to walk by His power. Like Peter, I had to be brought to the end of my strength so that I could learn to walk in His."

It was quiet for several moments, and then toward the back of the room, an elderly African pastor slowly rose to his feet. He addressed me in a quiet, resonant voice, speaking gently into the silence, "Brother, you have given us the answer."

The pastors did not crowd me afterward to shake my hand like a North American audience might. They simply got up and quietly left the hall. Lunch was coming up and we would soon be called to seat ourselves. As the crowd thinned out, another older pastor came and took me by the hand. "You must walk with me," he said and led me out through the compound along a dirt path bordered by lush foliage. As we walked, he began to speak.

"Here in Africa, we know what it is to struggle to follow God. The journey is hard and many fall on the path. What you have shared with us today is what we need to hear. You must write this in a book and send it to us. We need to know that we cannot serve God from our own strength. We need to know that He is faithful and will never let us go. This message will strengthen us for the task that lies ahead."

As we ended our time in Mwiki and prepared for our morning bus trip to the airport, one of our Tanzanian hosts came to me. Looking into my eyes with characteristic directness, he said, “You have saved one of us.” I did not understand and asked him what he meant. He told me that one of the pastors had come to the conference in the same state that Peter had been in. Like Peter (and I), he had not known how to ask for help. Unable to see how he could go on any longer, and unwilling to dishonor God with his failure, his plan was to come to the conference and say goodbye to his friends. Then he would go home and take his own life.

As this very broken pastor heard the story of a man whose faithlessness did not nullify the faithfulness of God, the Holy Spirit reached out to him. The realization that his service to God did not depend on his own ability and strength, but on God who was faithful, broke through his resolve. Reaching out to his friends, he shared where he was at. They gathered around him, praying for him and giving him the support that he needed. Having given his failures to God, he received the forgiveness and mercy that God so longs to pour out on His children, and he regained his hope for the future.

Questions:

• Do you have a relationship that is beyond your ability to fix or make right? Which one? What did it take for you to come to this conclusion?

• Where have you lost your idealism? How has it affected you?

• Have you committed a sin that you feel even God cannot forgive you for? Have you become bitter against God? How does the idea of simply accepting His forgiveness make you feel?

• Have you experienced “mercy”? Where? How?

Chapter 14

Now is the Time to Forgive

It is always the right time to forgive, even when it does not feel like it

"Therefore if you are presenting your offering at the altar, and there remember that your brother has something against you, leave your offering there before the altar and go; first be reconciled to your brother, and then come and present your offering."

Matthew 5:23-24

Tony and I had a falling out. I had known for some time that Tony was not one of my supporters. Cutting remarks and other signs of his dissatisfaction finally burst into open hostility at a staff retreat during a group exercise designed to measure the health of our leadership team. Part of the analysis included a time to share, in group, issues we might have with one another. We were encouraged to do so with sensitivity.

Tony did not know how to do that. He had internalized his real feelings for so long that they finally came pouring out of him in an attacking and derogatory manner. When his turn came, he sat motionless for several seconds and then began to spew his pent-up anger, telling the group exactly what he thought of me and why he felt I could never become the pastor that our Church needed. Abruptly, he ran out of words and the room sat quiet and shocked. That pretty much finished the exercise. Even our facilitator did not know how to pick up the pieces and move forward with the rest of what he had planned for the retreat. Tony and I left that meeting with something between us.

The aftereffects of that encounter stayed with me as the days went on, while things at work began to deteriorate. Nothing had been resolved and what had begun as a minor malfunction in our team now became a significant issue. I knew that I needed to talk to Tony but I thought I had better wait for the "right time."

Months went by and the "right time" never came. One Saturday morning, as I sat at my computer struggling to write a sermon, a thought came to me. I should go and speak with Tony. I toyed with the phone, knowing all I had to do was make one call and book a meeting with him, but it did not feel like the right time. I set the receiver back into its cradle. Nope. Definitely not the right time. I have since learned that forgiveness needs to be done now and that I cannot trust my feelings to guide me when it comes to matters such as this.

The thought would not go away. "Lord," I prayed, "it doesn't feel like the right time." Besides, I had to get my sermon finished. If I did not get that done, what would happen the next morning when I stepped up to speak to my congregation and found that I had nothing to say? Regardless of all my good reasons to put off talking to Tony, no relief came and I could not get properly focused on the message I was trying to write.

Finally I picked up the phone and dialed Tony's number. He answered immediately. Would it be okay for me to come over? Yes, it would. I got in my car and went. Tony met me at the door and led me into his living room. I sat down facing him and we looked at each other in silence as my mind blanked and all of the conversation starters that I had prepared on the way over suddenly disappeared. Gathering my resolve, I began, "Tony, I came to say that I'm sorry for what happened between us and I apologize for not coming to deal with this sooner."

It was as simple as that. No big long discussions about why he might have felt as he did. No long explanations about what I had meant and how he had misunderstood me. Just, "I'm sorry for what happened between us." Tony suddenly became quite animated and gave me a fairly lengthy and rambling response, the contents of which I have since forgotten. We closed the conversation and I left to head back to my office. The sermon seemed to come easily after that and Sunday morning, as I remember it, went quite well.

Something changed between Tony and me that day. He was no longer guarded when he spoke with me. In fact, he became one of my most committed supporters. I mentioned to him one day that I had noticed the difference and asked what had changed. He looked at me for a moment. "You showed humility," was all he said. A willingness to lay down my pride and take the initiative to apologize allowed God to do His work and had won the day. In thinking back on how obedience to God's prompting brought about such a positive outcome, I was struck with how, in my waiting for the "right time," I was really saying that I would go and deal with the situation when I felt like it. I had let my pride dictate my actions rather than doing what was most healthy, difficult though it may have been. Jesus' words came back to me: "Go, first be reconciled to your brother and then come and present your offering."

What I heard God saying to me was, "What are you waiting for? Do what you have to and leave the results to Me." It is easy to use feelings as a way out when we struggle with issues and offenses that we need to deal with. It is easy to over-spiritualize our emotions and equate God's leading with what we are feeling. Don't do it! Apologize now. Forgive now. Now is the time. Make the opportunity and get it done. Do not avoid it because of feelings. According to Jesus, when something is wrong between us and another party, the initiative to deal with it always lies with us. Taking action sooner rather than later will allow you to let go of what is past and to move forward into freedom. Paul says it well:

"...one thing I do: forgetting what lies behind and reaching forward to what lies ahead, I press on toward the goal for the prize of the upward call of God in Christ Jesus."

Philippians 3:13-14

Forgiving is always the most healthy course of action, as well as being the only option that lines up with God's Word, regardless of how we might feel at the moment. Chances are that, once we do what is healthy, our feelings will confirm that we made the right choice as God blesses our obedience with His peace. Forgiving someone does not mean that everything in life will suddenly become perfect, but it does mean that we will find ourselves able to move forward in a life-giving way on the journey that God has created us for. Keep in mind that the end of that journey will be heaven and that getting there is the process we are walking out day by day as we learn to forgive.

Adding the eternal perspective

Forgiveness has eternal consequences. The realization that viewing betrayal in light of eternity can dramatically reduce the power of those offenses to affect us, and thus make it easier to forgive, became real to me as I stood alongside my brother's casket.

We had known that Ian was dying. He had always been a happy presence, regardless of his struggle with the debilitating effects of cerebral palsy but, over the previous months, the light had gone from his eyes and he had become increasingly non-responsive to those around him. My desire to see him free of his suffering prompted me one Sunday morning to ask the people in my Church to pray with me that God either heal him or take him home. Some 250 people rose to their feet, joined hands, and prayed. Very shortly my answer came in the form of a phone call from my sister. She was characteristically straight to the point: "Boyd, Ian just died." Mom and Dad were visiting with us that week and I called them together around our kitchen table to share the news. The wheels were set in motion, funeral preparations begun, and the family started to gather.

On the day of the funeral, the casket lay open at the back of the Church for those who desired to come and view the body. As I approached Ian, I could see him lying with his head cocked at the slight angle that he normally had when asleep. Having spent so many years unable to move, his jaw muscles had tightened, making it impossible for the mortician to get his mouth to close, even in death. I touched his cheek, laying the back of my hand against the cold, hard skin and it struck me with new force that my brother was dead and that the body in front of me was an empty shell.

Not fully sure what I should be feeling, the memories flooded back as I stood beside him, simply experiencing the moment. Ian was diagnosed early in his second year with cerebral palsy and had been fully dependent on the rest of the family for his physical needs. All of us took an active role in caring for him. We fed him. We held him as he sat on the toilet. We bathed him as he lay on a small hammock slung over the bathtub. I was reminded of how I used to carry him outside to play in the snow caves I dug on the front lawn in the winter. Clutching the hood of his nylon snow suit, I dragged him behind me as we wormed our way through the tunnels. Though completely dependent physically, he had his full mental faculties and I would keep up a running conversation, reading his response from the expressions on his face and the way he moved his head.

I remembered putting him to bed on evenings when Mom and Dad were out. The pre-bedtime ritual that had developed between us often included a wrestling match and, being that Ian did not wrestle well, I wrestled for the both of us. With spastic limbs sticking out in all directions and after much thrashing and laughter, we would finally be ready for bed. I would position his bent little body for another night's rest by placing a pillow under his knees to prop them in place and arrange the covers so that he would be sure not to get cold in the night. Later in my teen years, after my own surrender to Christ, we added prayer to the evening ritual and, as I prayed, he would arch his neck back and look to the sky. His arms would rise spastically into the air as he prayed, his verbal expression taking the form of groans pointed towards heaven.

Standing alongside his body with my memories, I experienced something profound. Abruptly it seemed as though heaven stood open before me and I was enveloped by a deep sense of peace and love. In that moment, nothing else mattered. I knew Ian was gone and I knew that where he had gone was very good.

In those moments beside the casket, I suddenly found myself thinking of a close associate who had betrayed my trust. I found myself wishing that he was there. I would have thrown my arms around him, told him I loved him and let him know that what was between us was not important anymore. It suddenly struck me that, in the light of eternity, what had been done to me did not really matter. When my time came to die, I would not be taking the pain of the betrayals I had suffered with me when I went to heaven.

"Then I saw a new heaven and a new earth for the first heaven and the first earth had passed away, and there was no longer any sea. 2 I saw the Holy City, the new Jerusalem, coming down out of heaven from God, prepared as a bride beautifully dressed for her husband. 3 And I heard a loud voice from the throne saying, "Look! God's dwelling place is now among the people, and he will dwell with them. They will be his people, and God himself will be with them and be their God. 4 'He will wipe every tear from their eyes. There will be no more death' or mourning or crying or pain, for the old order of things has passed away."

Revelations 21:1-4 NIV

Jesus had looked at what was done to Him in light of eternity and had forgiven everything. In that moment the thought came clearly to me that, not only did my offenses have no eternal significance, but they only mattered within the framework of this life. I realized that if I could see what had been done to me in light of eternity, it could change everything. This insight was significant because it meant, if I changed the way I looked at offenses done to me from a "this life only" perspective to an eternal perspective, it would change the impact of those offenses on my life and reduce their ability to torment me. Think of it this way: a betrayal that destroys ten years of investment in a career or relationship costs much if we look at it from the perspective of someone who only expects to live for seventy or eighty years. Ten years out of seventy is a huge loss, but if we understand that God has made us for eternity, and view the betrayals we have suffered in light of that understanding, ten years lost from eternal life is nothing by comparison. By exchanging a temporal perspective for an eternal one, we can change the offense's value in terms of time and investment lost, making it easier to forgive those who have hurt us.

The three forgiveness focuses

There are three focuses of forgiveness for those seeking freedom from the effects of betrayal. The first is on forgiving others who have hurt us, the second is on forgiving ourselves for our own failings and the third is in regard to the anger so many of us carry toward God. We often have to apply forgiveness in all three of these areas rather than just in one or the other.

Forgiving others

Jesus made it clear that we must forgive those who have betrayed us when He placed forgiveness at the core of the Lord's Prayer and taught His followers to pray, "Forgive me, Lord, as I forgive those who have sinned against me" (Matthew 6:12). This may mean forgiving another individual, a corporation, an institution we have come to hate, even another people or religious group that we are prejudiced against for one reason or another. If peace of spirit, soul, and body eludes us, there is a good possibility that we are living with unresolved offenses. Regardless of who the focus of our anger is, if we are going to experience the freedom we were designed for, we need to learn to forgive those who have hurt us.

Forgiving Ourselves

Many people carry a sense of self-condemnation due to some kind of failure for which they have come to blame themselves. Condemnation morphs into self-hate and, after a time, living with it becomes our "normal." If we live with it long enough, it saps our energy like an open drain carries away water, leaving our lives dry of joy and coloring everything that we do. Some have lived this way for so long that they do not even recognize it anymore.

There are several kinds of people affected in this way.

For co-dependent people, self-imposed guilt comes with our failure to fix those around us. There is a whole demographic of people who take responsibility for the failures of others. Rather than recognizing that both parties in the relationship carry responsibility for their choices, we have tried to take the full weight of their failure, and ours, upon ourselves. This kind of guilt is common among parents or partners of addicts. We need to remember that even Jesus could not fix people who did not want help. If Jesus could not do that, then who are we to think we can? Better to deal with our responsibility and let the other party deal with theirs.

Some of us do not understand God's mercy and, until we come to the realization that God's desire to forgive us is greater than the magnitude of our failure, it can be difficult to accept His forgiveness. We expect justice and feel that we should not be let off the hook easily for what we have done. We believe that we must be punished before allowing ourselves to be forgiven. We have no real understanding of the unconditional nature of God's love and may not realize that it is a sin to refuse to forgive someone Christ died for – even if it is ourselves. Though we claim to believe in the God of forgiveness, regardless of what we say, our lives tell the true story of what we really believe.

Sometimes chronic self-condemnation can be an expression of demonic influence. Accusation and deceit are favorite tools of the devil. Often this kind of struggle is marked by an ephemeral, groundless kind of self-hate, the beginnings of which can be traced back to the certain situation from which it has been nurtured and grown. Counselling alone will not work for a person struggling with demonically exacerbated guilt because unforgiveness issues compounded by demonic bondage are not based in logic. In such a case, it is crucial to take the time to share the gospel with the affected person and then assist them in yielding the issue to Christ by helping them pray through the "repent and believe" process as they indicate a readiness to do so. Once the Spirit of God is given access to the issue, the demon's power is destroyed and the person can step into freedom. For someone who gains freedom from demonic power, all they may know is years of coping with that oppression. Once they gain their freedom, they will need retraining in how to develop new and healthy ways of living. It is at this point that good counselling and mentorship become vital.

Forgiving God?

A third focus of forgiving is in relation to God Himself. Blaming God has been a common practice throughout history, both by individuals and in the various cultures of the world. The first recorded instance of this is in Genesis 3 when Adam indirectly accused God of causing his problems by giving him a wife who caused him to sin. Has God actually done anything wrong to anyone? Although biblically the response must be "no," failed expectations and disappointment often turn into anger and we will need to deal with that in order to move forward.

Much if not all of our anger at God stems from our failed or unrealistic expectations of Him. All of us who follow God will have unrealistic expectations of God at some point in our faith journey. The issue we struggle with is one of control. Many times I have found myself praying a certain kind of prayer as I try to control how God leads my life: "Dear Lord, please bless what I want to do for You." Whether we are honest enough to openly admit it or not, when God either does not do what we want Him to do, or in the way we want Him to do it, we often become angry. Maybe He has refused to visit destruction on someone who treated us badly or who we feel deserves punishment. Maybe He simply has not given us the career track we wanted. Whatever it is, God often gets blamed for simply being a good parent because He does not say "yes" to everything we demand of Him. It has to be said that God will not give us what is bad for us, though we often ask for things that are not in our best interests (James 4:3).

Even Jesus' disciples had unrealistic expectations that Jesus did not live up to. They expected Him to call fire down from heaven and blast those who were treating them poorly. What they did not expect Him to do was to turn the other cheek and teach them to do likewise. They expected Jesus to choose favorites. They did not expect Him to wash their feet and then tell them to do the same to each other, nor did they expect to be told to repeatedly forgive those who repetitively hurt them. They saw Jesus the way they wanted to see Him rather than being willing to see Him for who He really was. Regardless of how it happens, failed expectations often lead to disappointment and regret. Jesus' disciples experienced that too, as their dreams of what Jesus would do fell apart at the cross and they went through hardship they had not planned on. When what they had pinned all their hopes on failed to materialize, the disillusionment that came with it was powerful and paralyzing.

Many of us struggle to think in terms of needing to forgive God. For some, even the act of questioning God may be seen as disrespectful, yet it is so much easier to come to grips with anger that can actually be addressed for what it is, rather than trying to deal with the effects of anger that is actively hidden and labeled as something else. The Spirit of God calls us to this kind of honesty.

If we can simply be honest about the fact that our walk with God has not been the way we envisioned it, we can get real with God and allow Him to lead us into freedom. For this to happen, it is vital that we give ourselves the permission to be honest with God and to ask the questions and share the doubts that we have experienced. If the prophets Jeremiah and Habakkuk could do it, we can, too. (Jeremiah 12:1-2; Habakkuk 1:12-17).

Without that transparency, our faith and service to God will become a veneer of fear and performance, preventing us from gaining the kind of closeness to God that we were created for.

Questions:

- How do you react to the idea of being angry at God?

- How have you reacted to disillusionment in your relationship with others? With God?

- Has this chapter given you any insight into what you need to do? What is it?

- How does seeing what has been done to you in light of eternity impact you?

Chapter 15

Finding the Offense

Step one: Diagnose yourself.

Getting honest is a prerequisite for any journey into finding the freedom that forgiveness can bring because without a good understanding of the problem it is impossible to take decisive action. As we come to confront the reality of what we have done and experienced, we are faced with a choice to do something about it. What follows is a diagnostic tool designed to help us begin that process by identifying the symptoms of unforgiveness in our own lives. The checklist below is based on the Apostle Paul's writings about the "deeds of the flesh," or indicators of self-centered living (Galatians 5:19-21). You will need some time and a quiet place in order to minimize distractions as you work your way through the list. If you recognize significant numbers of these indicators in your life, you may be struggling with unresolved offense. Begin by praying that God would open your eyes to see what you need to see and, as you go through each symptom, ask yourself if it is present in your life to an unhealthy extent. Understand that everybody will have had at least some experience of these indicators, but you are looking to see if these are thematic features in your day-to-day living.

Do you have:
Hatred of (There can be several focuses of hatred.)

__ self
__ another person. Who? ______________________________
__ an organization. Which one(s)?______________________
__ a racial group. Which one(s)? ______________________
__ a religious group. Which one(s)? ____________________
__ a tribal/national group. Which one?__________________

Jealousy (Jealousy is often a trust issue. I may be jealous and protective of my relationships, unable to trust because I was "dumped" by a friend or lover in the past. Or I may be jealous of those around me who have good relationships while I do not.) I am jealous of:

__ my spouse;
__ my friend(s)lifestyle;
__ my friend's property/possessions
__ Other ________________________________

Envy (This means dissatisfaction with what I have. It can cause anger at those who have what I want or cause me to betray and hurt others in my striving to get what I want.)

__ I want what someone else has. (Name it.)

Revenge

__I have the desire to punish someone or get back at them.
__I am actively looking for opportunities to pay someone back.

Strife (I have someone in my life that I cannot stand being around. Name them.)

Anger (There are several kinds.)

__ Outbursts of anger (This is aggressive anger. I am explosive and intimidating.)
__ Smoldering/silent anger (This is passive anger. I punish through giving others "the silent treatment.")
__ Suppressed anger (This is passive anger. I have been coping for so long with the anger of others that I have not realized I am angry, too.)
__ I was trained that I have no right to be angry.
__ I was trained that it is a sin to be angry.

Disputes/arguing

__ I cannot allow myself to let go of an issue.
__ I use arguing as a way of keeping people at a safe distance.
__ I regularly pick fights with those around me.

Dissentions/factions/taking sides

__ I easily take offense on behalf of others (co-dependency).
__ I have a "me/them" mentality.
__ I look for the negatives in others.
__ I am always suspicious of others' motives.

A sense of failure

__ I failed myself.
__ I failed at something – work/a responsibility/life. (Name it.)
__ Someone failed me. (Name them.)
__ I feel God failed me.

An ongoing sense of disappointment over failed expectations

__ I feel disappointment in myself.
__ I feel disappointment in someone else. (Name them.)
__I feel disappointment in the way life has worked out to this point. (In what way?)
__ I feel disappointment in how God has moved or not moved in my life. (In what way?)

Depression that began with a betrayal, failed relationship, or personal failure (Name the situation.)

__ A low sense of personal worth (possibly stemming from a betrayal or a relational trauma and the associated, unresolved guilt)
__ I have actively humiliated/shamed myself. (Name what happened.)
__ Someone else has actively humiliated/shamed me.

__ A sense that I have been treated unfairly or betrayed by someone
__ Someone did not give me what I felt I deserved.
__ Someone did something to me that I felt I did not deserve.

An obsessive need for fair treatment

__ I obsess over how unfair my life is.
__ I spend time thinking of how badly I have been treated. (By whom? When?)
__ I spend a lot of time justifying myself to others (even in my head).
__ I obsessively replay conversations in my head as I rehearse what I should have said.
__ I spend an inordinate amount of time going over and over an offense in my mind.
__ Thoughts and feelings of self-pity over certain events spool in my mind constantly.
__ I obsess over certain situations and how they should have been handled.

Ongoing emotional pain over a failed relationship

__ I cannot seem to move on.
__ The memory of an old relationship stays fresh with me, even though I am in another relationship.

A tendency to avoid

__certain people
__certain places because of whom I could run into there (If you check this it means you are avoiding someone. Name them.)

A sense of having been actively used or betrayed by

__ myself
__ someone else (Name them.)

__ an organization (Name it.)
__ a people group (nationality, political, religious, tribal, or racial group) (Name it.)

Having these symptoms may indicate that you are carrying unforgiveness, and the willingness to change the way you have handled those who have hurt you is an absolute requirement. A mentor once told me that there can be no freedom without the willingness to change. Without that willingness, you will remain on the same road of life, handling the same issues the same way you have always handled them while striving to manage the pain these issues have always generated. Repenting of the old ways of coping and replacing them with a new way is critical if you want your quality of life to change. The next step is to get specific about those whom you need to forgive.

Step two – Making your list

1. Who has actively betrayed you or simply let you down? Who are you disappointed with? These are the people you need to actively forgive. Make your list. For this section include people, yourself, and organizations. (We have a section on God coming shortly.)
   a. ______________________________
   b. ______________________________
   c. ______________________________
   d. ______________________________
   e. ______________________________

2. Use a sheet of paper for each person you listed and write out what you need or want from them. What are the things that, if they did them, would make you feel ready to move on? (These are the "conditions" that you have on the relationships and hanging onto them can prevent you from being able to move on. More on "conditions" soon.)

3. Look at your list of demands and ask yourself: "Am I ready to release them?" If you are ready to take the risk of trusting God with your situation, and the pain associated with it, you must be willing to pray deliberately with the intention of letting the person go. Remember that your words only mean what your heart puts into them, so get ready to pour your heart into the words as you hand them to God in prayer. That does not mean you have to feel good about praying what you need to pray. It just means you need to be deliberate and mean what you are saying to God. Feelings are a by-product of your choice to forgive. Make the choice and the feelings will come later as the freedom that forgiveness brings begins to take effect.

Step three. Ask yourself: "What is my unforgiveness costing me?"

What is it costing you in order to hang onto your grudge? Oftentimes what has been done to us has been so huge, and stolen so much from us, that the sheer size of the offense prevents us from thinking in terms of what it is costing us. It can be more expensive than we realize in terms of what we trade away as we struggle to keep our pride and sense of fair treatment intact. Look at what you have been exchanging in order to hang onto your offense and ask yourself what carrying this sin/offense has cost you. What have you lost because of it? Have you been trading away a relationship, intimacy, peace, or joy for the sake of holding a grudge? Work your way through the "cost list" below.

This offense has cost me:

__ A relationship with a mother/father/husband/wife/child/friend/etc. (Name it.)
__ Friendship. The price being paid is measured in loneliness.
__ Finances. A split relationship costs money as assets are divided and lawyers have to be paid. (How much?)

__ Family. A split relationship has set family members against each other.
__ A home. This means more than a "house; it is a place to belong.
__ Time with children. A marriage split has removed time with, and access to, children.
__ Community. This can include Church, a club, sports team, and/or any kind of social gathering of friends and family.
__ Peace of mind. This is the ability to relax and focus on the moment.
__ Personal trauma. This is the freedom from torment over a past event.
  __ Self-punishment can be a way of keeping the trauma alive.
  __ Avoidance. Fear of confronting the issue to resolve it can keep the trauma alive.
__ Sense of belonging. This has been lost along with the relationship in question.
__ Unity and the sense of strength and peace that comes with it.
__ Trust. Sometimes the ability to trust is given up as we protect ourselves from further hurt.
__ Anger. Holding onto a grudge and obsessing over it keeps us angry. We have to guard against getting our identity from our anger. Would you identify yourself as an "angry person"?

The list above is not exhaustive. What else can you think of? Write it out.

With these "costs" in mind, ask yourself whether or not holding onto this offense is worth it. Are you ready to move into freedom? If you decide the offense is not worth the cost of hanging onto it, proceed to the next section.

Step Four: Remove the conditions – Renouncing our agenda in favor of God's will.

By placing conditions on your willingness to resolve the offense you carry, you effectively refuse to entrust your situation to God. By letting go of your conditions you allow God to bring His strength to bear on your behalf. This next tool is the "conditions list." These are the demands we have that block us from forgiving and attaining our freedom. As you read through this list of conditions, think of situations where you find yourself saying, "Lord, if You do this for me, then I will trust You by forgiving and moving forward."

List the conditions/demands you have on God that must be met before you are willing to take the step of faith to forgive and move on.

Section 1 refers to conditions we may have set on forgiving other people and trusting them to God.

I will forgive:

__ if ____________ apologizes. (Name the person.)

__ if ____________ makes things right. (Name the person and what needs to be made right.)

__ if ____________ returns what he took from me. (Name the person and what he took.)

__ if ____________takes back what she said about me. (Name the person and what was said.)

__ if God makes those who hurt me pay. (Pay in what way? How do you want them to suffer?)

__ if I get back what I have lost. (What have you lost?)

__ if I can only get fair treatment. (Describe the "fair treatment" you need.)

__ if people can know what has been done to me is not fair. (Who do you need to know this?)

__ if I can be justified in the eyes of others. (Justified means "seen as innocent.")

Section 2 refers to the conditions we may have set on forgiving ourselves and being willing to receive God's forgiveness.

I can forgive myself:

__ if no one knows about what I have done.
__ if I can keep my life, along with my problems, private.
__ if I can keep up my image. (Describe the image you need to maintain.)
__ if I can keep ________________ between You and me. (Name it.)
__ if I can perform for God/another person/myself the way I want to/need to. (Are you ready to renounce your need to control the way your resolution will look?)
__ if my faith can stay private.
__ if I do not have to ask for help. (I am ashamed other people will know what I have done and that I cannot fix it myself.)
__ once I have earned it.
__ once I have punished myself enough.

Section 3 deals with conditions we may have placed on letting go of our anger at God. Think of a petulant child talking to his/her parent as you go through this.

God, I am ready to trust You:

__ if You fix my child's/my spouse's/my friend's/my situation.
__ if You heal me. (Of what?)
__ if You give me my business back.
__ if I get the job I want.
__ if You pay ________________ back for what he/she did to me.
__ if You will give me the blessings I want.
__ if I can be in control of _______________. (Name the situation or relationship).

__ if You act like a loving God should act and bless the lifestyle/ choice that I want You to bless.
__ if You give me my way.

These lists are not exhaustive. Add other conditions/demands that come to mind:

____

____

____

Having identified your conditions and demands, the question you want to ask yourself next is whether you are willing to let them go?

Willingness and conditions

The story of the rich young ruler, as recorded in Mark 10:17-27, speaks of an encounter between Jesus and a wealthy young man who was concerned about where he would go after he died. The young man came to Jesus to ask for eternal life, but it soon became clear that he wanted it only as long as he could have it on his own conditions. He wanted both eternity and his self-centered lifestyle, too. The story says that Jesus looked at him, loved him, and, with the truthfulness and compassion that characterized all of Jesus' dealings with people, addressed the very heart of the young man's struggle. Jesus let him know that he could not have both a selfish life here and life in eternity as well. He had to let go of one if he was going to have the other. This is not a story against money. It is a story about surrendering our conditions and choosing to trust God with the outcome. After weighing what such a choice would cost him, the young man could not do it and turned away, choosing his wealth and a lifestyle tinged by the fear of death over becoming a follower of Jesus.

Taking the risk to trust God is at the core of forgiveness and if, for any of the above reasons, you find yourself holding out on trusting God, it will block your ability to move forward in the freedom that could otherwise be yours. Even Jesus could not help someone who was not ready to be helped. Look back at what you have learned about yourself through the exercises you have just finished and ask yourself: "Am I willing to change?" You must come to the point of being willing to forgive without conditions. If you are willing to trust God with your conditions, move to the next section.

Chapter 16

Praying the Process

It is time to learn how to pray through what you have discovered. Find a quiet place so that you will not be interrupted. I encourage you to write out your prayers so that you can deliberately and systematically pray through what needs to be given to God. You can either pray in stages as you work your way through this next chapter or craft the whole prayer and then take time to pray it all through at once when you are finished. Though we will be using a structured approach in order to help us be deliberate about how and what we pray, structure is not the same as a formula. One of my mentors liked to say that there are no "magic" prayers, meaning that prayers spoken as formulas or incantations do not change people. Only the Spirit and power of God can truly change lives as honest, heartfelt prayers communicate our surrender to God and allow Him to do His will in us.

Begin by praying: Lord, send Your Spirit and empower me to pray what I need to pray. In Jesus' name. Amen.

Next we pray for God's power. When we forgive, we enter the realm of the miraculous and we need the Spirit of God to empower us so the miracle can happen.

Continue praying: Lord, let Your kingdom come into my situation. I am at Your mercy, in Jesus' name. Amen.

Next we pray for God's agenda to replace our own. By now, we have identified who has hurt and disappointed us, along with the conditions and demands that have been holding us back from resolving the offense we are carrying.

In this part of the prayer, we tell God that we are ready to let Him do things His way and we ask for His power and participation.

Pray: Lord, I am ready to do this Your way. You know the demands I have placed on those who have hurt me. I now confess and renounce the conditions that have kept me from forgiving. (Name what you have placed on your "conditions list" for each person you are forgiving). I am ready to forgive and trust my situation with ____________________ to You, Lord, in Jesus' name. Amen.

Renouncing your weapons

We may need to renounce our weapons. The Apostle Paul says in 2 Corinthians 10:4-5 that our weapons are different than the weapons the world uses. Very simply put, this means that we cannot treat others as they have treated us because it is just another way of paying them back and creates more offense than ever. In order to renounce your weapons, you have to identify what they are. Gossip, manipulation, and accusations are some that are common in our world. Take a sheet of paper, focus on one of the situations where someone betrayed you and begin to write out a description of how you handled yourself. Asking the following questions will help you to focus your writing:

1. What were your immediate reactions to those who hurt or offended you? Did you react selfishly? How? Did you withdraw? Did you go on the attack and, if so, in what way? Did you gossip, become defensive, reject them back, or simply begin to avoid them? Write it out.

2. What did you do in order to try to get the outcome that you wanted? Write it out.

This exercise can take brutal honesty to do well because it does not spare your pride. The greater the honesty, the better equipped you will be to take action and make the necessary changes. Do this exercise several times and pull the results together onto one sheet of paper. When finished, set down your pen and leave it for a few hours. Often, as we take time to allow our thoughts to settle, greater clarity will come as our mind sorts and categorizes itself. Once you have had an adequate break from writing, come back and read over what you have written.

Begin writing now…

Take your break now…

As you read over what you have written, look for patterns of punishment and selfishness that show a focus that is more about getting what you want than it is about healing the relationship you are struggling with. Can you recognize the behaviors that have become your "weapons" as you struggle with relationships gone wrong? Are you willing to renounce using them, so that God can give you another way of handling your pain as He leads you to a deeper level of maturity?

If you find yourself struggling with hatred for a person who hurt you, take time to deliberately think about their value in God's eyes. You may need to ask forgiveness for hating someone Christ died for. Remember that forgiveness is about granting mercy, regardless of how unfair things might seem. This applies to self-forgiveness as well. If you find that you have hated yourself for the failures of your own life, take time to meditate and realize your value in God's eyes, keeping in mind once again that it is a sin to hate someone Christ died for, even if that someone is yourself. Be mindful that every time we forgive we take another step toward deeper maturity. The more mature we become, the more we are able to trust God and the less our lives will be dictated by our circumstances and emotions.

Whoever you have hated or held unforgiveness against, put their name in the blank of the prayer below and pray it deliberately.

Pray: "Lord, forgive me for not seeing ____________ as You see him/her/me. Give me Your perspective that I may see him/her/myself with Your eyes. I forgive ________________ for _____________." (Go through your list of what this person has done to you.)

Next, pray to remove your conditions and demands on forgiving the person you feel has hurt or betrayed you. Understand that you are not saying that what they did was right but you are releasing them into God's hands for Him to deal with. Be deliberate about renouncing the "payback" you have wanted. Go back to the conditions list and methodically pray through what you have made note of, with the intent of letting these things go.

Pray: "Lord, I put ___________ into Your hands and I release him/her/them from my demand that he/she/they ___________________________ make things right/apologize/acknowledge what they did/etc. (Fill it out according to your conditions list.)

What if God leads you to talk to them face to face?

Once you have finished praying this part of the prayer, you may have a sense of leading to go and speak directly with the person you have just prayed about. I have often been asked if we need to approach everyone who has hurt us face to face in order to either declare or ask for forgiveness. There are a couple of good reasons behind doing so and my response is "sometimes." The first is that it helps us grow in our maturity as we take responsibility for our part in resolving the struggle. The second is that we get to bring a blessing to the other party through our apology or declaration.

It is important to know that God does not ask us to apologize as a form of punishment. I was forced more than once to apologize to my sisters when I was a child. I do not remember being taught why it was important, just that it was required. It was humiliating and only resulted in deepening my bitterness against them and against my parents as well. Though for a time we can force certain behaviors, we cannot legislate heart change or healing for a broken relationship (1 John 4:18). Rather than being a form of punishment, a face-to-face apology is an expression of the surrender we have made to God and a demonstration of our desire to bless those who have hurt us (Luke 6:28). It is an act of mercy.

Actually facing a person and making an apology can be difficult. Being structured and deliberate can help. A simple process is to book an appointment in a place that has enough privacy so that you can speak openly. Pray before you meet with the other person. Ask God to open both of your hearts to hear what will be said. It may be a good idea to take some time and write out what you want to say. By taking a script, you keep yourself on track and you say what you want to say. It helps prevent the stress of the situation from derailing you from your intended purpose. Though it might not look as spiritual as you would like it to, being spiritual does not come from what you look like in terms of smooth presentation. True spirituality comes from a heart that wants to be true before God and others.

To start with, simply share what you have come to forgive. Include a statement asking for forgiveness for anything you have done that has been hurtful and let the person know that there are no strings attached. Keep it as simple as possible without trying to explain too much, because too many explanations can sometimes cloud the issue. Explaining can be done later if need be. Close the conversation by letting the other party comment if they need to.

How do I pray to forgive myself?

To forgive yourself, you must be ready to accept that God loves you and be willing to let yourself "off the hook." Unless you do this, you will find yourself holding onto self-hatred, believing that you are not worth what Christ did for you on the cross. Understand that God has already forgiven you and that when Jesus said on the cross, "It is finished," your forgiveness was accomplished. Remember to look at things in the light of eternity by comparing what happened to you with what happened to Christ on the cross. It helps to change your perspective and can make it easier to receive what you need to receive.

Pray: Lord, help me to forgive myself.

Do not stop with praying, "Lord, help me to forgive myself." Continue by praying to receive what you have asked for. Often people just pray the "help me" prayers, constantly asking and never receiving, even though the gift of forgiveness sits right in front of them waiting to be appropriated. Remember that Jesus said, "He who asks receives" (Matthew 7:8). Asking and receiving are two sides of the same coin and we need to pray both.

Go on to pray: Lord, forgive me for not forgiving myself. I now forgive myself for Your sake and I accept Your forgiveness for not accepting Your grace before this. I now accept the full forgiveness of my sins and renounce all self-punishment and self-hatred. I accept that You took my punishment on Yourself so that I could be free. I take my stand in the freedom You have given me and reject the work of the enemy and his attempts to get me to live in self-condemnation. In Jesus' name. Amen.

Adding the eternal perspective

If you need to add the eternal perspective to the situation you are praying for, pray: Lord, forgive me for not seeing this sin in the light of eternity. Forgive me for not realizing what is at stake here. I accept my forgiveness and I release myself/the other person into Your hands and ask You to bless me/them and call me/them to You. In Jesus' name. Amen.

Praying to forgive God

What do you do when you feel that God has failed you? Maybe you are one of those people who is disappointed in the way your walk with God has turned out. You are angry and you do not feel it has been fair. Maybe you were trained never to question God and, because of your training, you have packed away the many years of disappointments and failed dreams until you have lost all of your enthusiasm for following God. Though you give God verbal respect and attend Church regularly, if you are going to be honest about it, your walk with God is pretty empty.

We have to deal with our anger over failed expectations so that our relationship with God can be brought back into a healthy place. We need to let God be God and make the decision to trust Him with what we carry inside. Hebrews 4:13 (NIV) says that: "Nothing in all creation is hidden from God's sight. Everything is uncovered and laid bare before the eyes of him to whom we must give account." That means we are really just making the choice to be honest about what God already knows. Freedom from disappointment and anger at God come as we get real with Him, taking seriously the promise of God not to condemn us (John 3:17; Romans 8:1).

The first choice to make is to take the risk of being honest with God. If you are willing to do that, then ask yourself:

Am I angry at Him for failing me? __ Yes? __ No?

Am I angry at Him for not doing things the way I wanted them done in my life? __ Yes? __ No?

Letting God be God

Ask yourself, "How do I feel God has not met my expectations?" Write each item out. Be specific. The greater the honesty, the greater access you give God to what has bound you and the easier it will be to receive freedom from your anger.

Pray: Lord God, my relationship with You has not been what I expected it to be. I have carried these disappointments in my heart and I have blamed You for them.

Write them out. Use more paper if you need to.

1. ______________________________

2. ______________________________

3. ______________________________

4. ______________________________

5. ______________________________

6. ______________________________

7. ______________________________

If you are ready to let go of your anger toward God, read the following prayer. Decide whether it says what you are ready to say, and then go ahead and pray it. If you want to expand it, feel free. Remember that words are like a bucket and convey what you put into them. Use them to give God what is in your heart.

Pray: Dear Lord, forgive me for wanting to act as though I am my own God. Shall the pot say to the potter, "Why did You make me like this?" (Romans 9:20). Yet that is exactly what I have been doing. Lord Jesus, I now lay down my rights to run my life my way even as You laid Your rights down when You went to the cross (Philippians 2:5-8). I say that my life is now Yours. I give You all that I am and all that I have. I renounce my conditions on how You may guide and direct my life and I say, Jesus, that I trust You. I invite You into the places where I have carried disappointment over how You have worked in my life or where I have demanded my own way and I receive Your forgiveness for my anger toward You. I give You my future and bless You for what You will do with me. In Jesus' mighty name, I pray. Amen.

Having finished the prayers, it is time to look at re-engaging the relationships.

Adding action to your prayers

Once you have prayed, continue by re-engaging the relationships. It often takes more work to re-engage a relationship with someone we have had to forgive than it does to just find another relationship and start afresh. That said, it is important to re-engage, even though that may mean we have to actively resist the temptation to walk away. Moving on after forgiving can either be a means of veiled punishment, indicating an incomplete forgiveness, it can be simple laziness, or it can come from a fear of having to trust again. Whatever the reason, opting out of the relationship may save us some work and discomfort, but it will also cost the kind of intimacy and freedom that we yearn for because depth of intimacy is what re-engagement brings.

Christ refused to forgive and walk away. He lived out His conviction that His friends and family were worth more than their failings and demonstrated that re-engaging is the foundation for rebuilding the love that has been lost. We may claim to have forgiven but, if we drop the relationship easily and without attempting to re-engage, we are not doing what Jesus did. When the guards were sent to arrest Jesus in the Garden, there was a brief exchange and a short tussle, after which all of His disciples ran. With their fear so strong that it eclipsed their commitment to Him, each of them proved themselves unworthy of His love for them. Yet Jesus not only forgave them, He sought each of them out in order to show them that He still wanted their friendship. By doing so, He demonstrated that they were more valuable to Him for who they were than for what they had done and He took the relationships deeper than they had been before.

If we are willing to follow Jesus' example and press through the offense to forgive and re-engage with those who will allow it, we will find deeper intimacy, too, in the relationships we regain. But, if moving on is our practice, we will be forever doomed to a cycle of going back to the shallows and starting over while the intimacy and depth that we seek continues to elude us.

What if the other person is not open to re-engaging? Though Jesus re-engaged relationships with those He forgave when at all possible, it is not always possible. If that is the case, we are free to forgive and move on. We cannot make someone respond if they do not want to. Even Jesus could not force people to love Him.

Being proactive

Make no mistake about it, re-engaging can take a lot of effort and some types of relationship require a more proactive approach than others. For example, in a marriage, there is often more pressure to forgive and re-engage than there is in a friendship. The vows, presence of children, or the existence of common property are all factors that may push people to come back together when without them it would have been much easier to simply move on. Casual friendships usually do not have the depth of commitment that marriages have and that lack makes it easier to move on and start new friendships rather than working to resurrect old ones. Still, forgiveness is foundational to long-lasting friendships and, when the choice is made to forgive and re-engage a friendship that has broken down, the end result will be a deeper relationship. It takes effort but the rewards are well worth it.

Sometimes we are called to forgive even when there is no relationship to go back to. In cases where the other person may have died, all you can do is forgive them, honor their memory, and let them go. In one instance a number of years ago, a woman called saying that she had seen the promotional material for the Forgiveness Seminar and was going to be in town that weekend for the pre-trial hearing of the person who had murdered her family member. She did not know the person, having had no connection with them other than the impact they had had on her life when the crime was committed, so there was no relationship to re-engage, but she felt she might benefit from what we were teaching. I encouraged her to come explore what it could look like to forgive her family member's killer and it was helpful to her. In such cases, all you can do is forgive and leave that person in the hands of God, while you move forward yourself.

What about when the other person cannot be trusted? For those of us who have experienced betrayal, re-engaging means more than just choosing to trust again. It means that we need to learn to trust wisely. If you are an abuse victim or have a co-dependent personality, beware the temptation to allow the other party to continue to abuse your trust, because it makes you their partner in the evil that they are doing. Learn to say "no." If you choose to re-engage the relationship and you know the other person is not able to handle the level of trust you previously gave them, be careful. Jesus told his followers to be "wise as serpents, and harmless as doves" (Matthew 10:16 kjv), meaning that we need both a realistic understanding of the people we are dealing with as well as the ability to set godly boundaries in our relationships with them. Learning to trust wisely is a growth curve we are all on and allows us to love while at the same time placing limits on the behavior of those who may not be able to love us back in the way we would like them to.

Remember that your aim is a healthy relationship, rather than simply protecting yourself from the other person, because whenever self-protection becomes the goal we tend to push people to a distance and short-circuit our ability to become intimate with them.

However you approach it, re-engaging entails a conscious choice and deliberate follow through. Jesus deliberately re-engaged life with those whom He forgave because He wanted the deeper intimacy that was to be gained by doing so. One of the biblical names of God is "Redeemer" and His promise to us is that, as we take seriously the call to forgive those who have hurt us, the pain we have gone through will not be wasted (Isaiah 48:17). God can, and will, bring something good out of what has happened to us, if we will trust Him to do so.

Freedom can be abused

Just as forgiveness lays the foundation for lives of freedom, so our choices either enhance our freedom or detract from it. We can use our freedom responsibly and live in increasing freedom as a result, or we can abuse our freedom and lose it. That does not mean we do not make mistakes – stupid and repetitive mistakes even – but we should not be deliberately selfish about doing so. Galatians 5:13 says, "For you were called to freedom, brothers; only do not turn your freedom into an opportunity for the flesh, but through love serve one another." 1 Peter 2:16 tells us to act as those who are free but not to use our freedom as an opportunity to justify doing evil things. The writers of these two passages of scripture warn us that mistakes are normal but we cannot make a practice of abusing the love we are given and still expect our relationships to grow.

A forgiveness lifestyle does not fear making mistakes. What would happen if parents who, for fear that their son would abuse his driving privileges, refused to allow him to get his driver's license? Doing so might keep him out of trouble on the road but it would also prevent him from growing into the maturity of adulthood. They would run the risk of ending up with an adult child living in their basement for the rest of his life. I smashed up the car shortly after getting my license and, when my dad got the repair work done, he handed me the keys again, along with some coaching. What I am saying is we all need the freedom to make mistakes, because making mistakes is a part of the journey of growth. It is in the crucible of experience that we learn to use our freedom wisely.

Forgiveness means that we need no longer live as victims of the pain and anger of failed relationships. Through forgiveness, God heals our brokenness so that we can move forward into restored freedom. God's strength brings hope and empowers us to move through situations rather than getting bogged down and stuck in them.

Forgiveness means saying "yes" to God's call to love and being willing to deal with others His way rather than the world's way. When we forgive, we demonstrate that our need for freedom has finally eclipsed the importance of punishing those who have hurt us, and getting fair treatment is no longer what is most important. Forgiveness means we have come to see our enemy as someone who has worth in the eyes of God and our situation as something God wants to redeem. We have glimpsed something of the heart behind Jesus' words when He said:

"Love your enemies and pray for those who persecute you..."

Matthew 5:44

At the end of the day, forgiveness brings us the freedom to grow in our intimacy, both with God and others, and calls us deeper into maturity as we make the necessary choices rather than just the ones that "feel" right. Forgiveness teaches us what it means to live redemptively. Sin does not get the last word. Mercy does.

Epilogue: Walking in ongoing freedom:

If you have decided to forgive, you will need to be proactive in both keeping and deepening the gains you have made. The insights that follow will be helpful toward consolidating the new lifestyle God has called you into.

Forgiving and re-engaging will give you much deeper relationships than you have ever had before. Remember that forgiveness means making your relationships more about what you can give than what you can get. Your freedom is not something for you to spend on yourself alone but is intended to transform you into the blessing to others that God created you to be. A selfish focus is the quickest way to bring a relationship to an end. Bring 100% of yourself to the relationship rather than just 50%. Beware of isolating yourself to protect from future betrayal and pain by making the choice to re-engage relationships when at all possible.

A forgiveness-based lifestyle is a realistic lifestyle. You need to accept that there will always be people who will fail you, including yourself. The only one who will not fail you is Jesus and He will not always do what we think He should. Because of His love for you, along with His determination to lead you into a healthy lifestyle, He will do what He must to lead you into the freedom that forgiveness can bring you. He will do this even to the point of leading you through difficult circumstances where you will learn to make the choices that need to be made. Be deliberate about identifying unrealistic expectations of Jesus and renouncing them. Allow your expectations of Him to be re-formed, if necessary, by your study of His Word in the context of a healthy community of faith.

Forgiveness will both call and allow you to be increasingly real with others. For those of us who live with unrealistic demands on our relationships, the disappointment of having our expectations fail repeatedly is often the source of our anger. It is important to replace unrealism with realism by identifying where you have been expecting unrealistic things of your relationships and repenting of these. Developing deeper relationships will include regular renunciation of selfish expectations of God, of yourself, and of others while asking Jesus to give you His perspective on those you are in relationship with. Make use of the opportunities and do it.

Growing deeper in your freedom requires active devotional reading and prayer. Take time with God in order to allow His Spirit to continue to keep your heart free. "Where the Spirit of the Lord is, there is liberty" (1 Corinthians 3:17).

Be aware of demonic counter attack. Be on guard for the old thought patterns and take your thoughts captive to Christ regularly. Stand in Christ. Resist the devil's work by standing in the power of God (2 Corinthians 10:3-5; Ephesians 6:10-17; James 4:6-7).

Grow in wisdom. Learn to trust wisely. Actively set healthy boundaries in your relationships. Do not demand of people what they cannot give, and, if your experience with someone shows that they cannot be trusted, be careful.

Get rid of the reference points that draw you back to the hurt of past experiences or to the "good old days" so that you can move forward. One example would be to destroy the old love letters that connect you with a failed relationship. It will help you avoid returning to the old victim mentality and minimize the temptation towards self-pity and/or picking up old grudges. Let go of the past and look to the future by placing past failures under Jesus' blood. Move forward into new relationships. Put yourself into God's hands and do not look back except to learn from the past. Keep what you have learned!

Find a mentor and be ready to accept their advice. Look for someone who has been through betrayal and who understands what it means to have to forgive so they do not steer you selfishly. Once you have found such a person, ask them to mentor you. Let their experience and coaching help you grow. Do not be proud, but be humble, ready to receive advice and to apply it. As you apply their advice, take time with them to process what you learned in the application.

Finally, be aware of your tendency to fall into old cycles and repent of the old habit patterns! Take action to break the old unhealthy cycles you have made for yourself and actively replace them with new and healthier ways of living. Make the choices necessary to change from a reactive lifestyle to a proactive one.

With forgiveness as the cornerstone of your lifestyle, you no longer need to just survive. You can live!

Notes

1. Webster's New College Dictionary 3rd Ed., page 448

2. Rwanda: Living Forgiveness, DVD

3. Narcotics Anonymous; Basic Text sixth edition, page 31

4. Schindler's List, The Movie

Bibliography

1. Webster's New College Dictionary 3rd Ed.
   Boston; Houghton Mifflin Yarcourt Publishing Company, 2008

2. Rwanda; Living Forgiveness DVD Video
   Copyright 2004, Agape International
   Producer Tom Sommer
   Distributed by Crown Video www.crownvideo.com

3. Narcotics Anonymous; Basic Text sixth edition
   Chatsworth; Narcotics Anonymous World Services, Inc., 2009

4. Schindler's List, The Movie
   1993; directed by Steven Spielberg; co-produced by Steven Spielberg, Gerald R. Molen and Branko Lustig.
   Amblin Entertainment. Distributed by Universal Pictures.

5. 5. Webster's ninth New Collegiate Dictionary.
   Copyright 1983; Merriam-Webster Inc.
   Published by Thomas Allen & Son Limited. Markham, Ontario.
   Page 1040